THE EMPIRE CITY

SONGS OF WELLINGTON

ANDREW LAKING

THE EMPIRE CITY

SONGS OF WELLINGTON

PAINTINGS BY BOB KERR

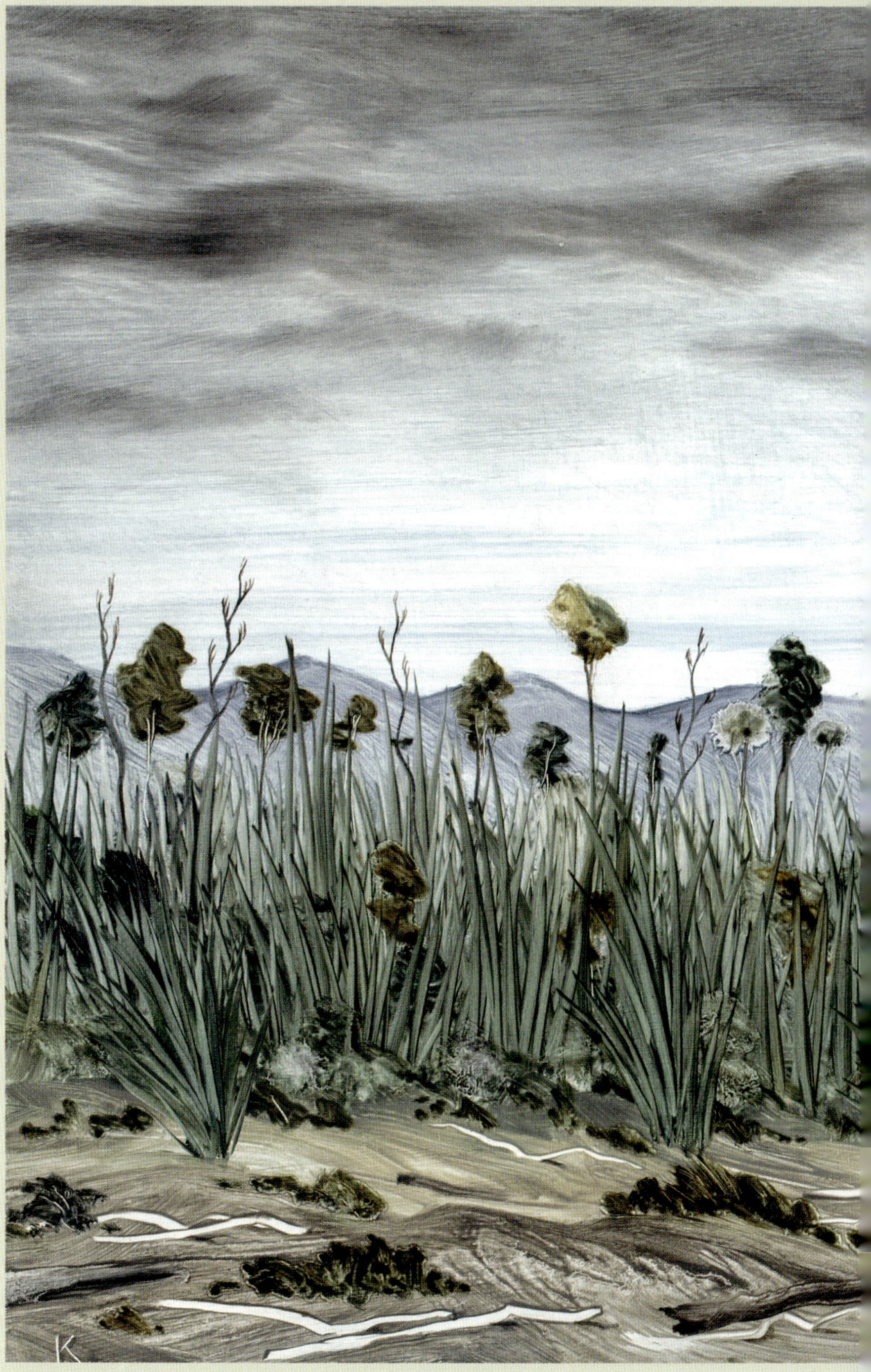

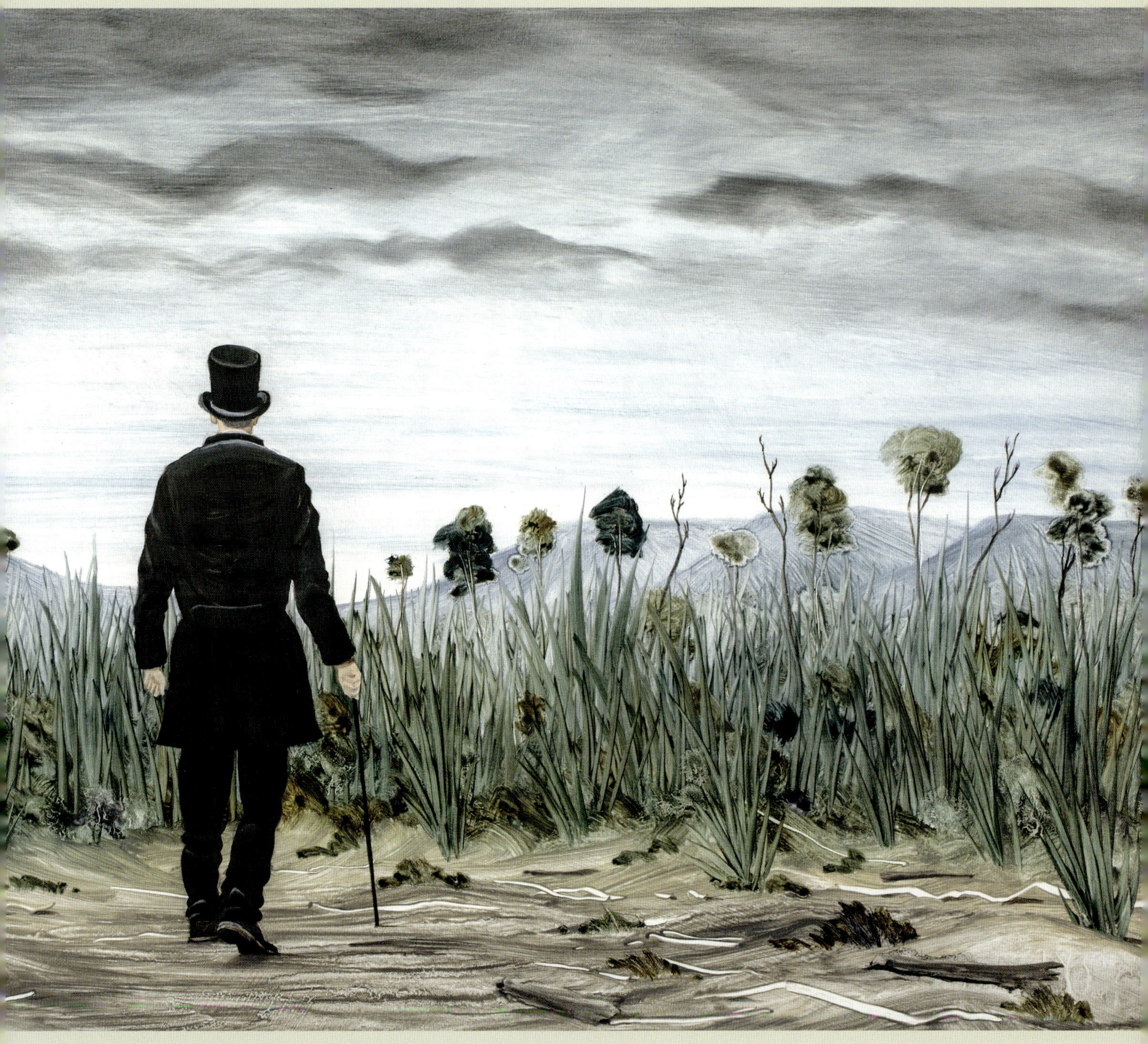

SONGS

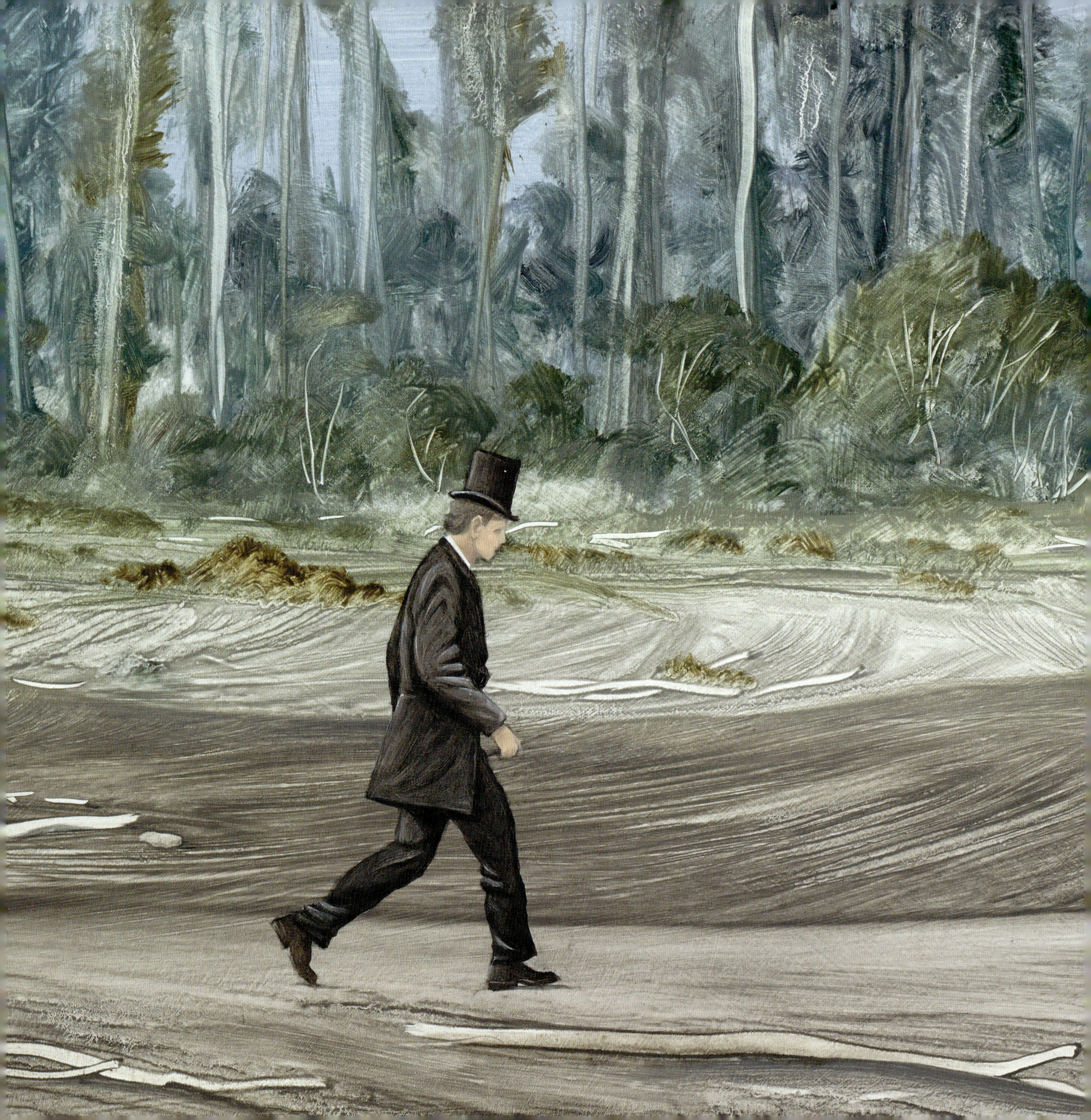

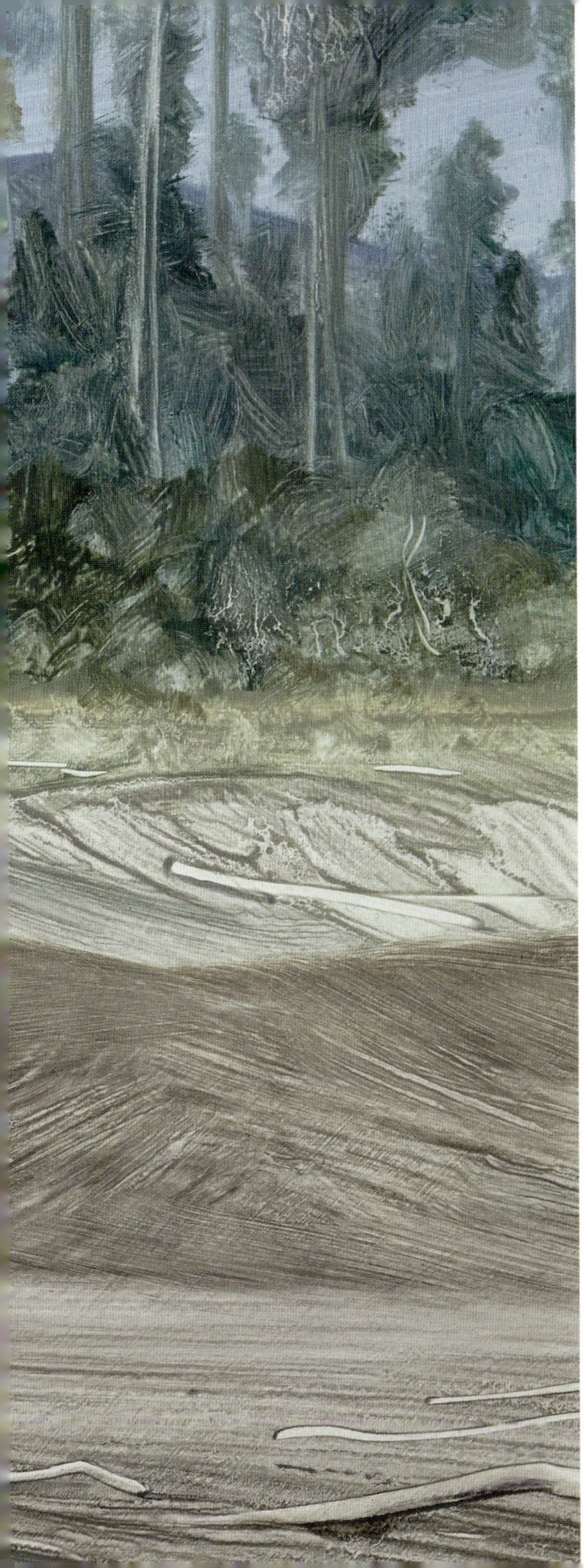

THE COLONIST

William Wakefield arrived in Wellington from London in 1839, employed by his older brother Edward to manage the New Zealand Company, buying large tracts of land from local Māori and selling them to European settlers with the idea of creating a new, model English society. He came with the burden of his past: a criminal record, army service, the death of his wife and separation from his daughter. Things would only get worse with the death of his brother and near impossible nature of managing a colony without the blessing of the British government in the severe isolation of early colonial New Zealand.

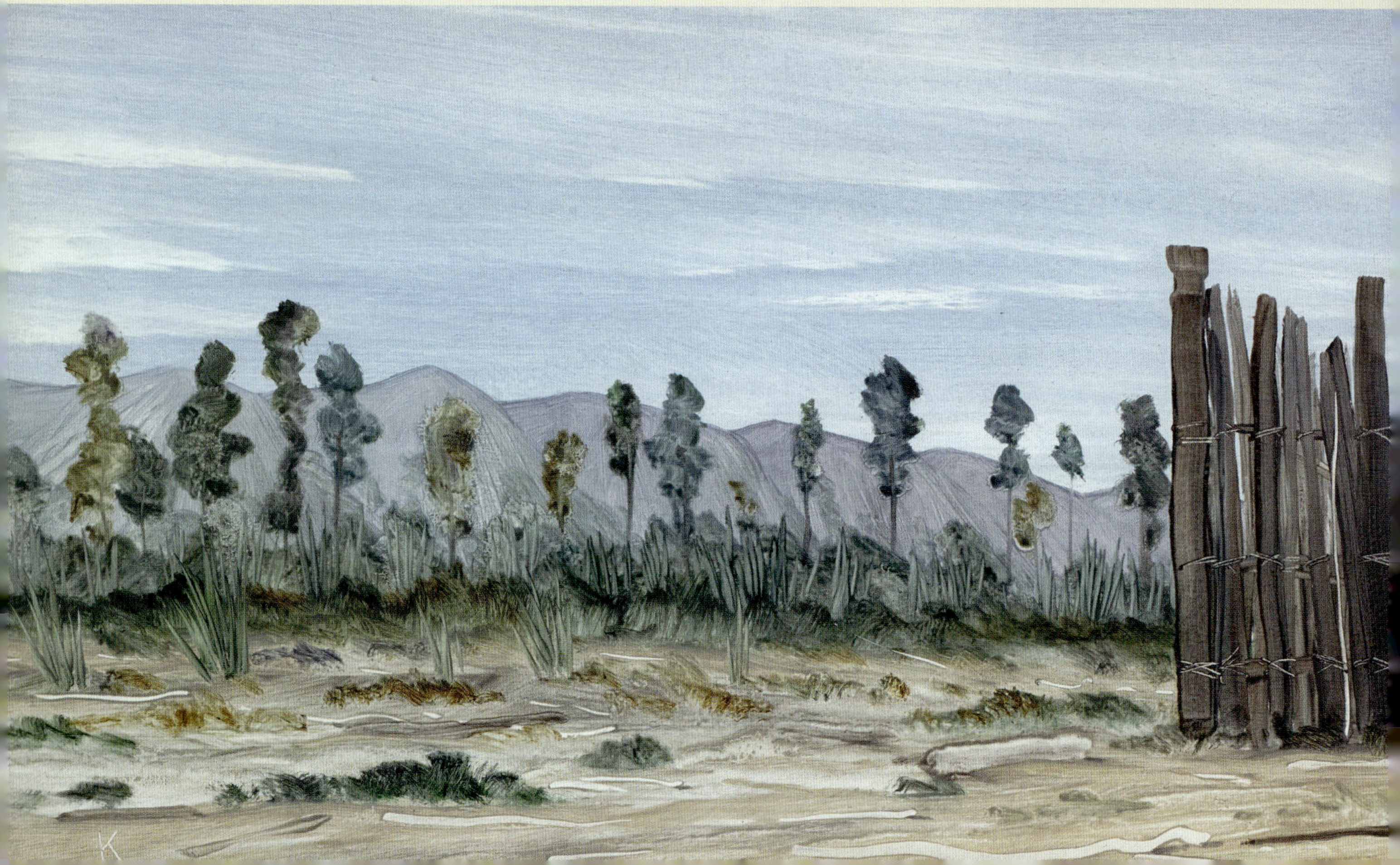

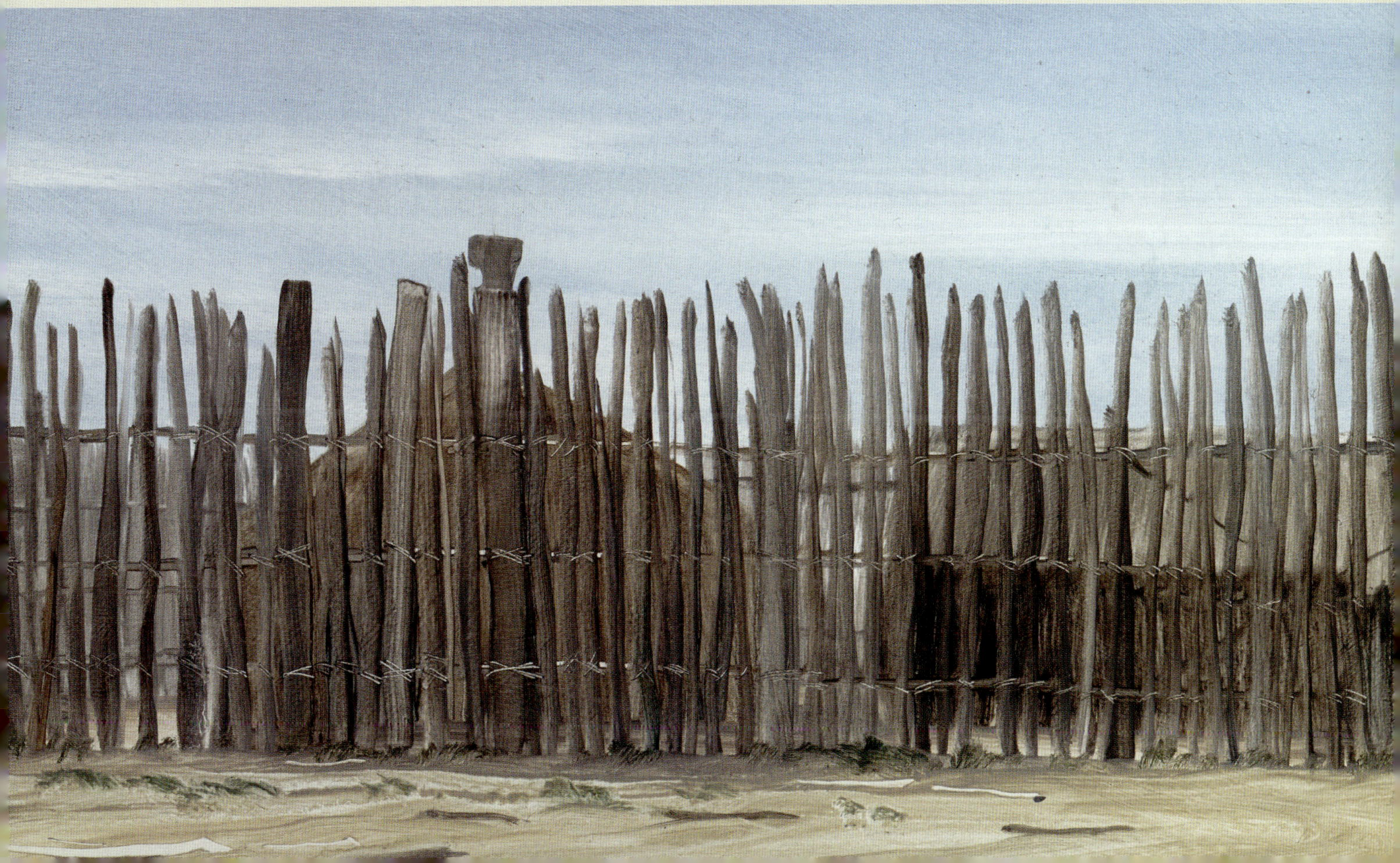

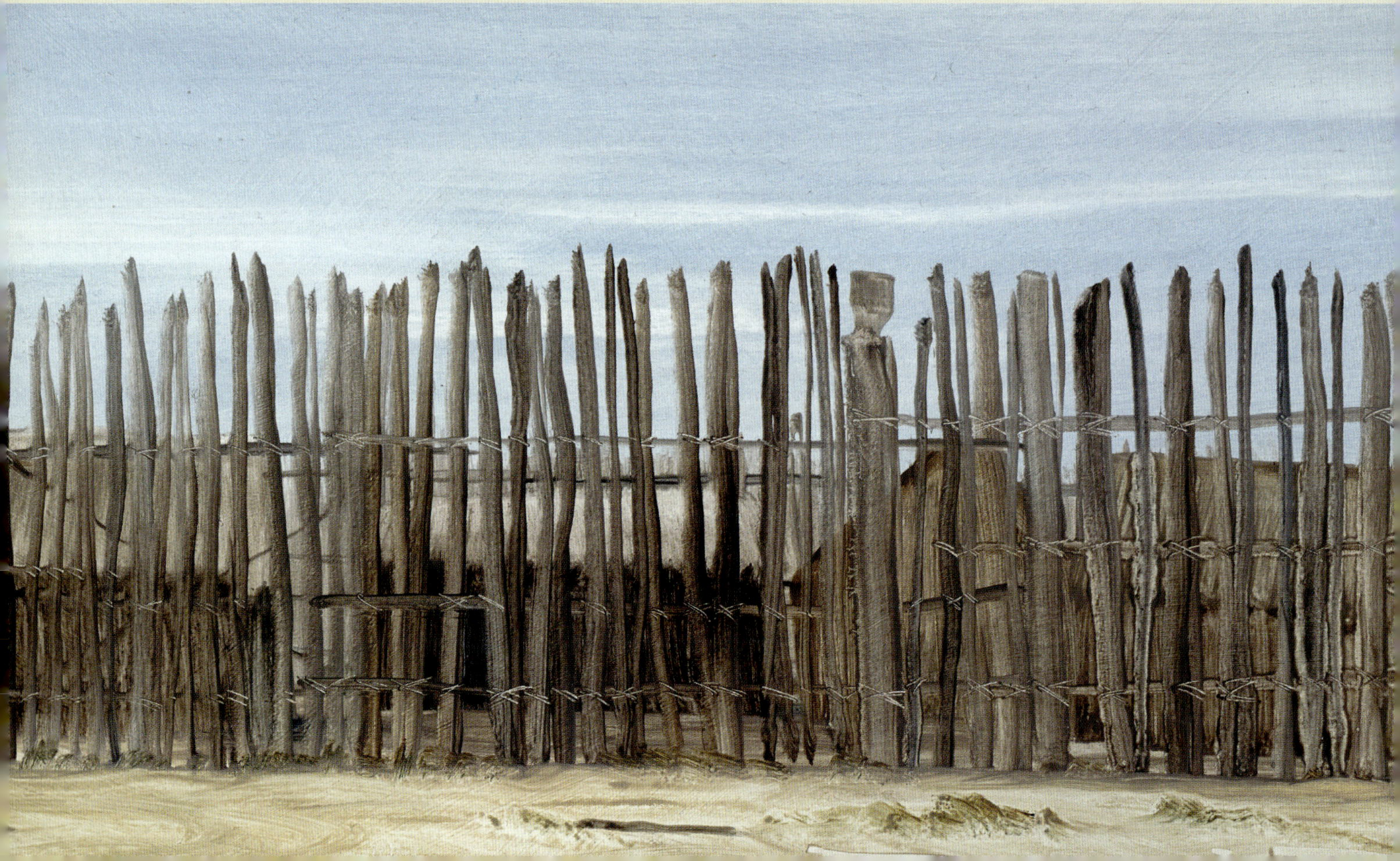

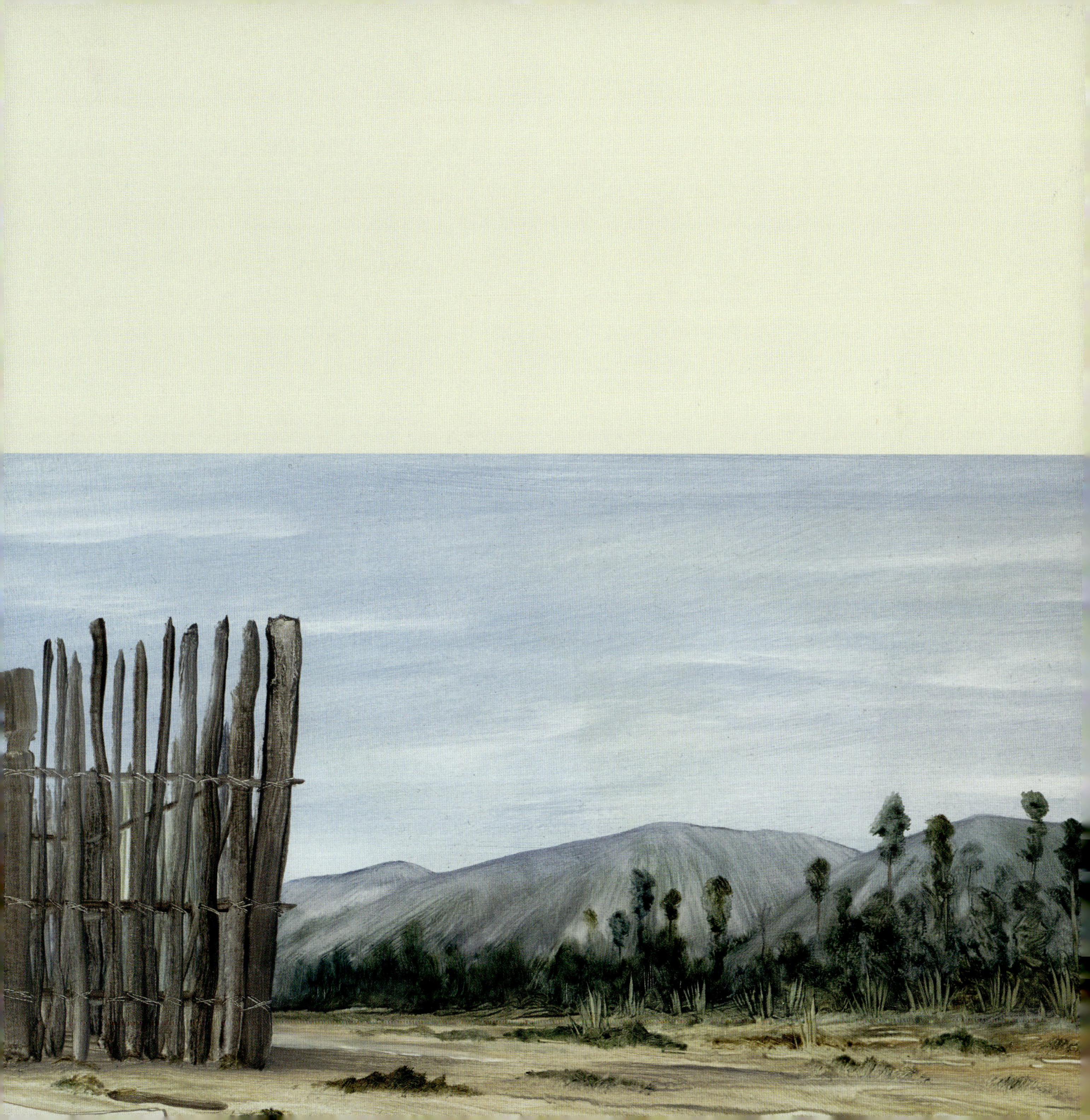

1. The Colonist

A cold mannered man, he sailed from London town
On the 4th of May, 1839
With a flowing cravat
A Chesterfield coat
And a chevron moustache

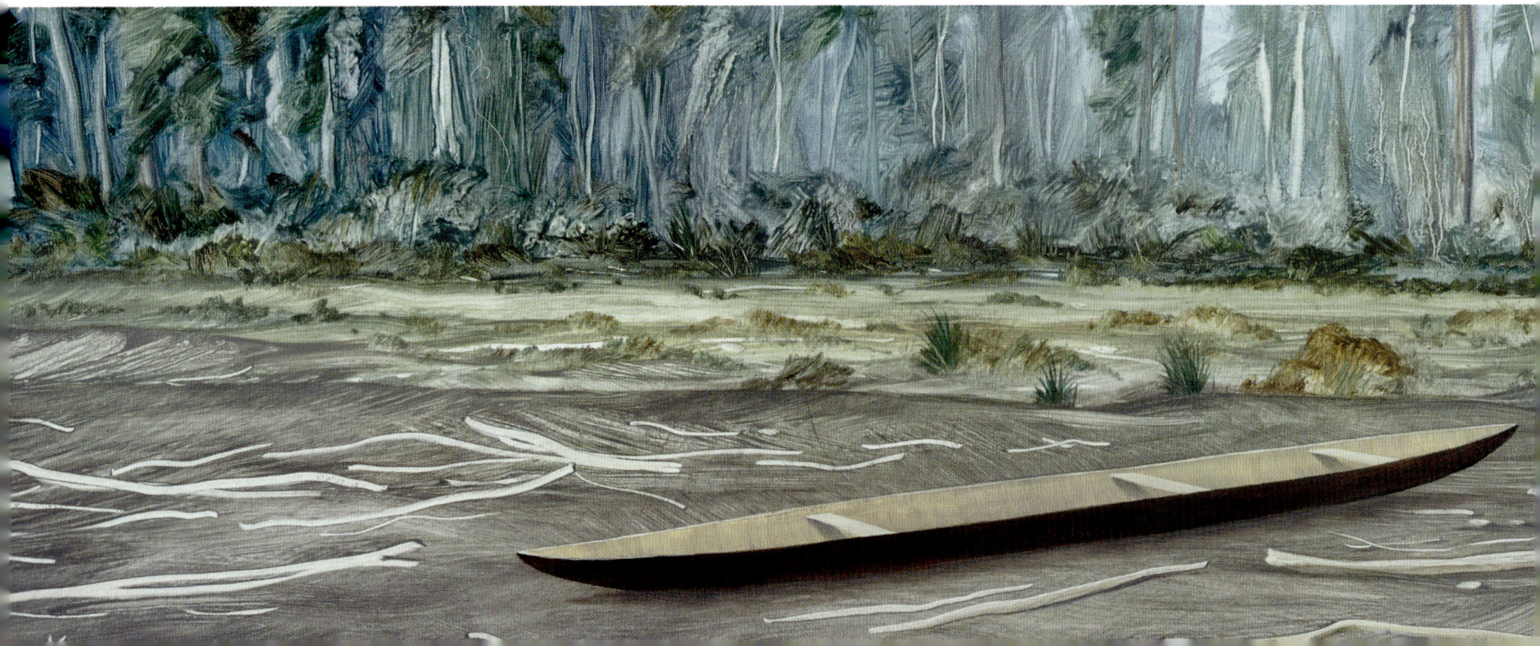

Struck by the mountains that trail on forever
Caught by the cold shadows at Ship Cove in winter
Sent by the company, left his family
And his conviction in the motherland

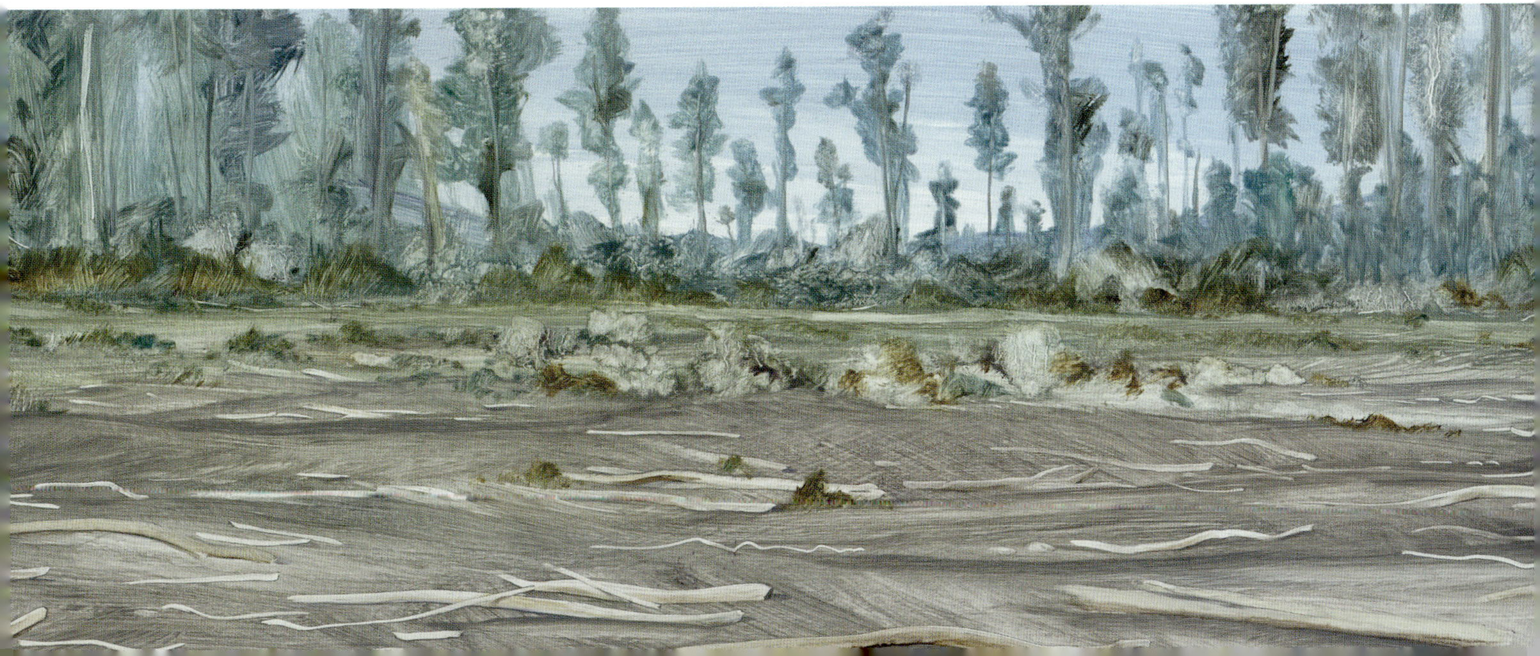

Buoyed by the wind he arrived on the quay
Looking for land for the company
Sixty-five thousand hectares for odds and ends
His coat fair covered his heart

He pushed aside those who'd welcomed him
Was pushed by settlers, tied by the motherland
Well you can call for your brother, but he's gone in Wairau
Call for the infantry, you won't find it
Call for Fitzroy ...

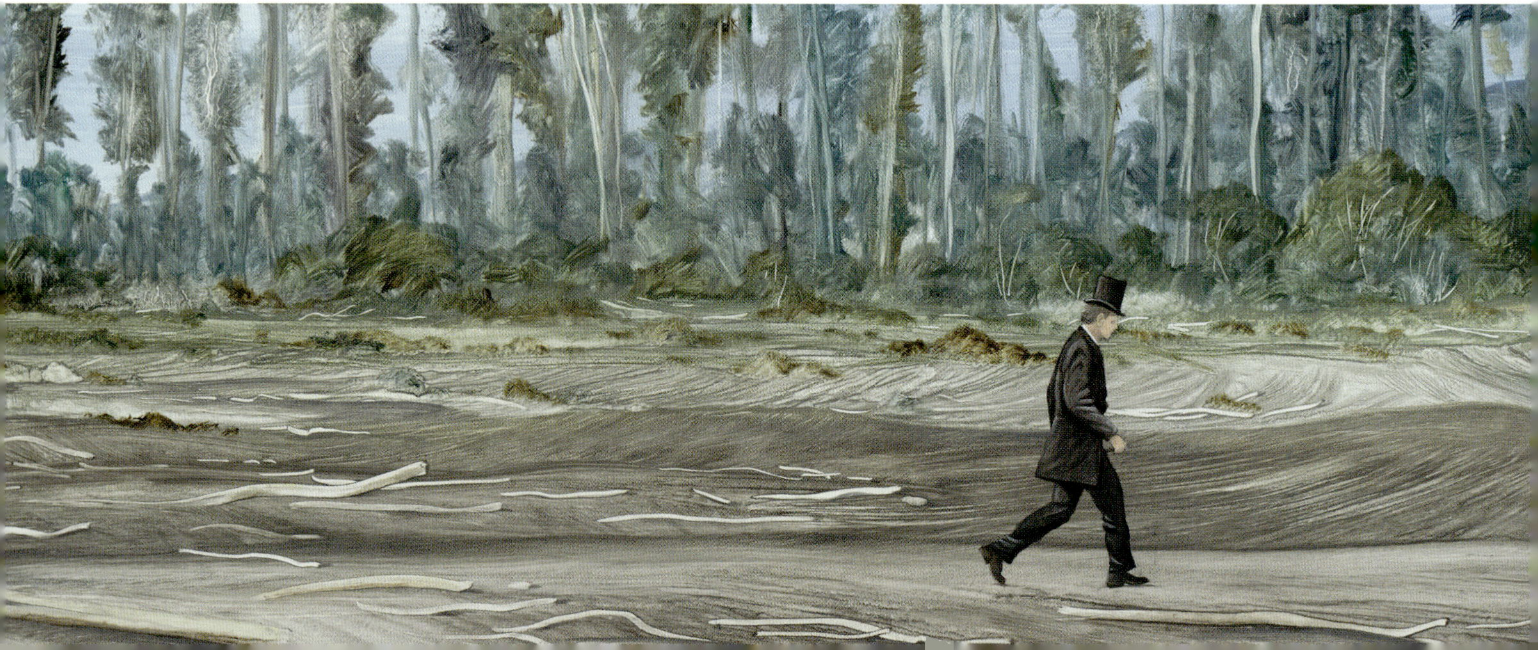

Six black horses led a gold-trimmed carriage
The women dressed in black crêpe gowns
Watched by the city all manner of people
So was the funeral of William Wakefield
The cold mannered man from London town.

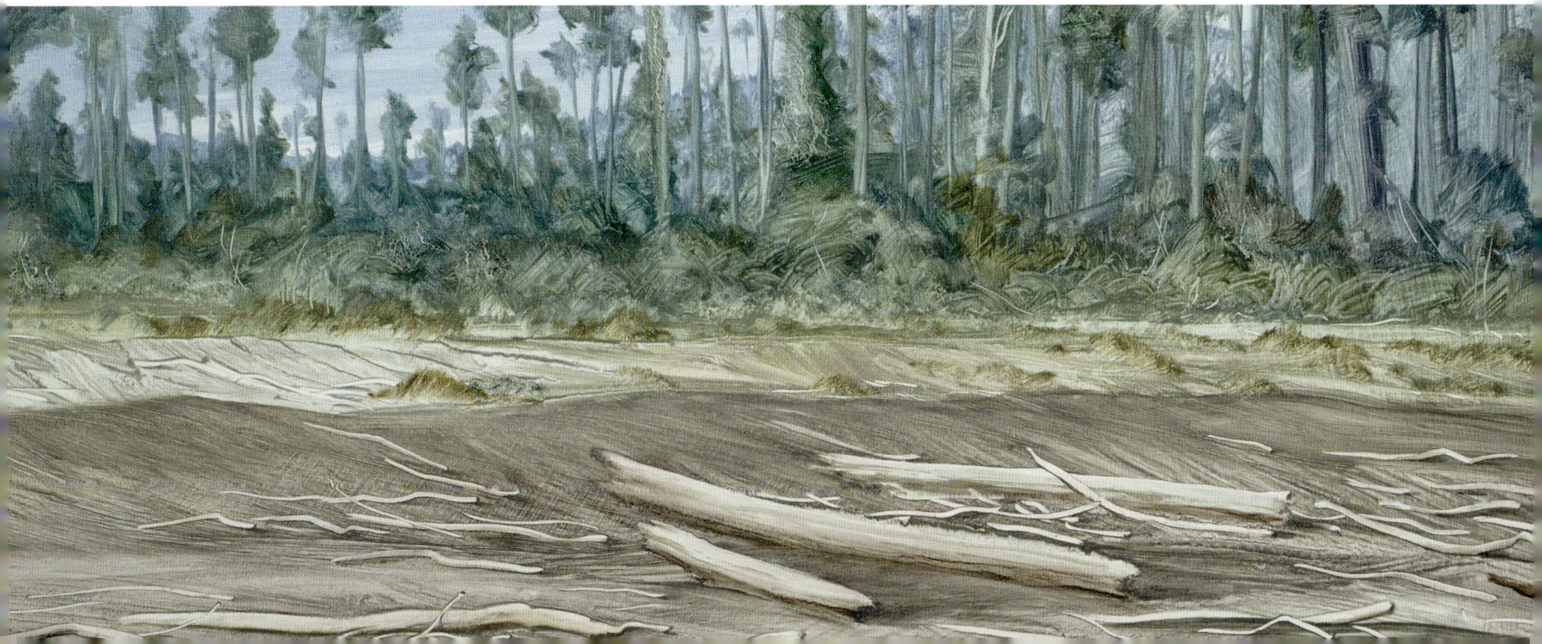

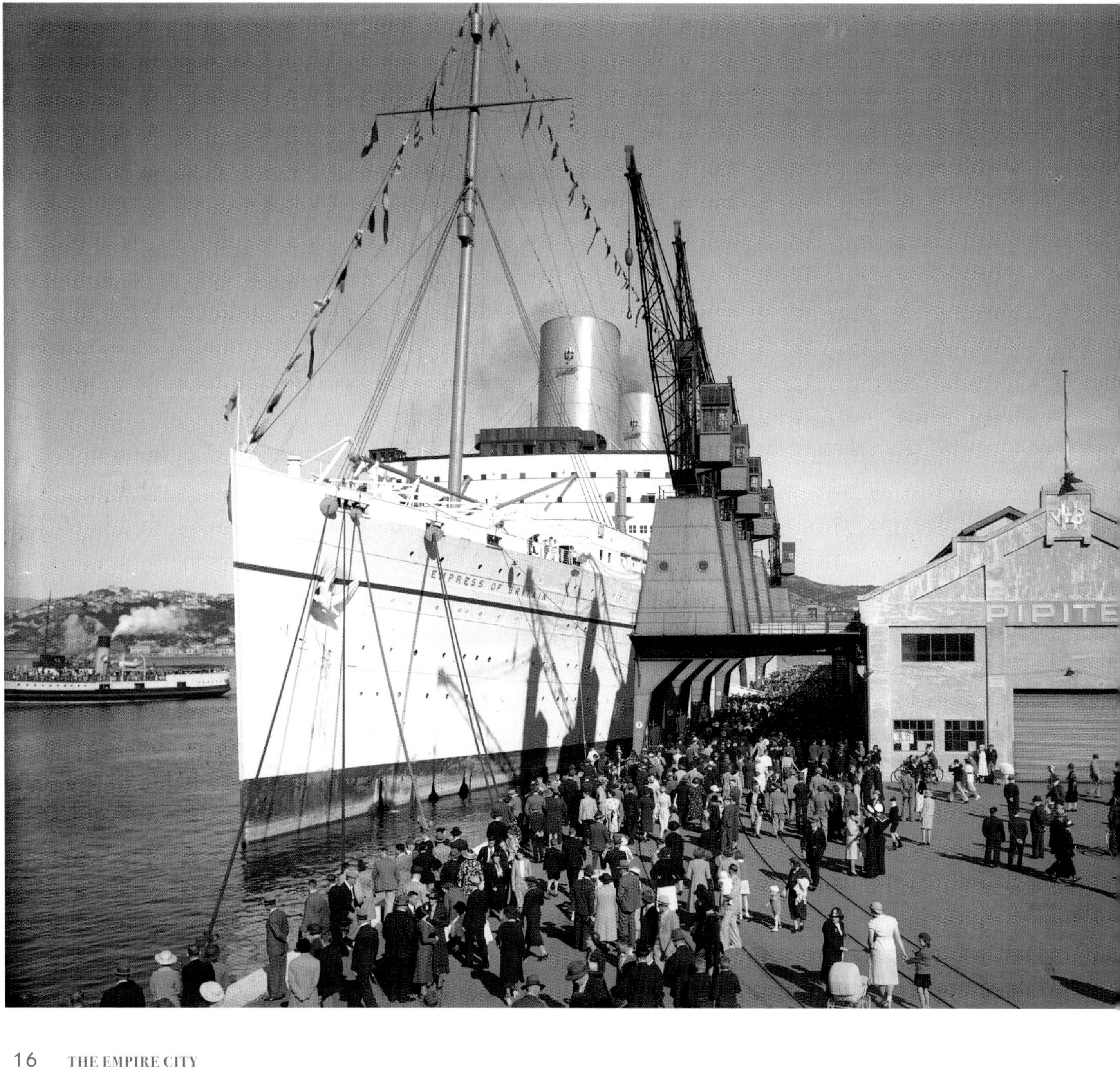
EMPRESS OF BRITAIN
PIPITE

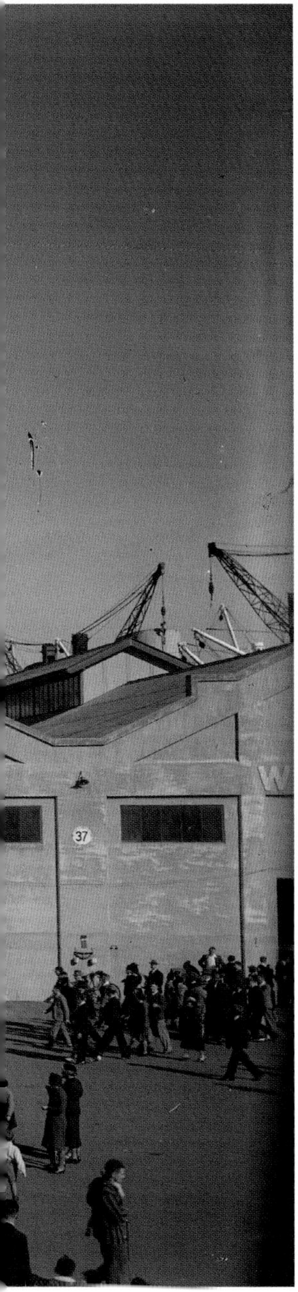

AT THE WHARVES

Wellington's modern waterfront has been developed to bring new life to the historic wharf area, bridging city and sea. But it is teeming with ghosts. Lives were played out on the wharves: fortunes were won and lost, thousands of ships came and went, millions of tonnes of goods were laboriously hauled on heavy rope slings in and out of vessels. People worked, fought and died here in the cause of trade, commerce and workers' rights – political struggles that sometimes dictated the course of the entire country. Now, although the port ships more goods than it ever did, the atmosphere and drama is gone, almost entirely mechanised and confined to the old North end.

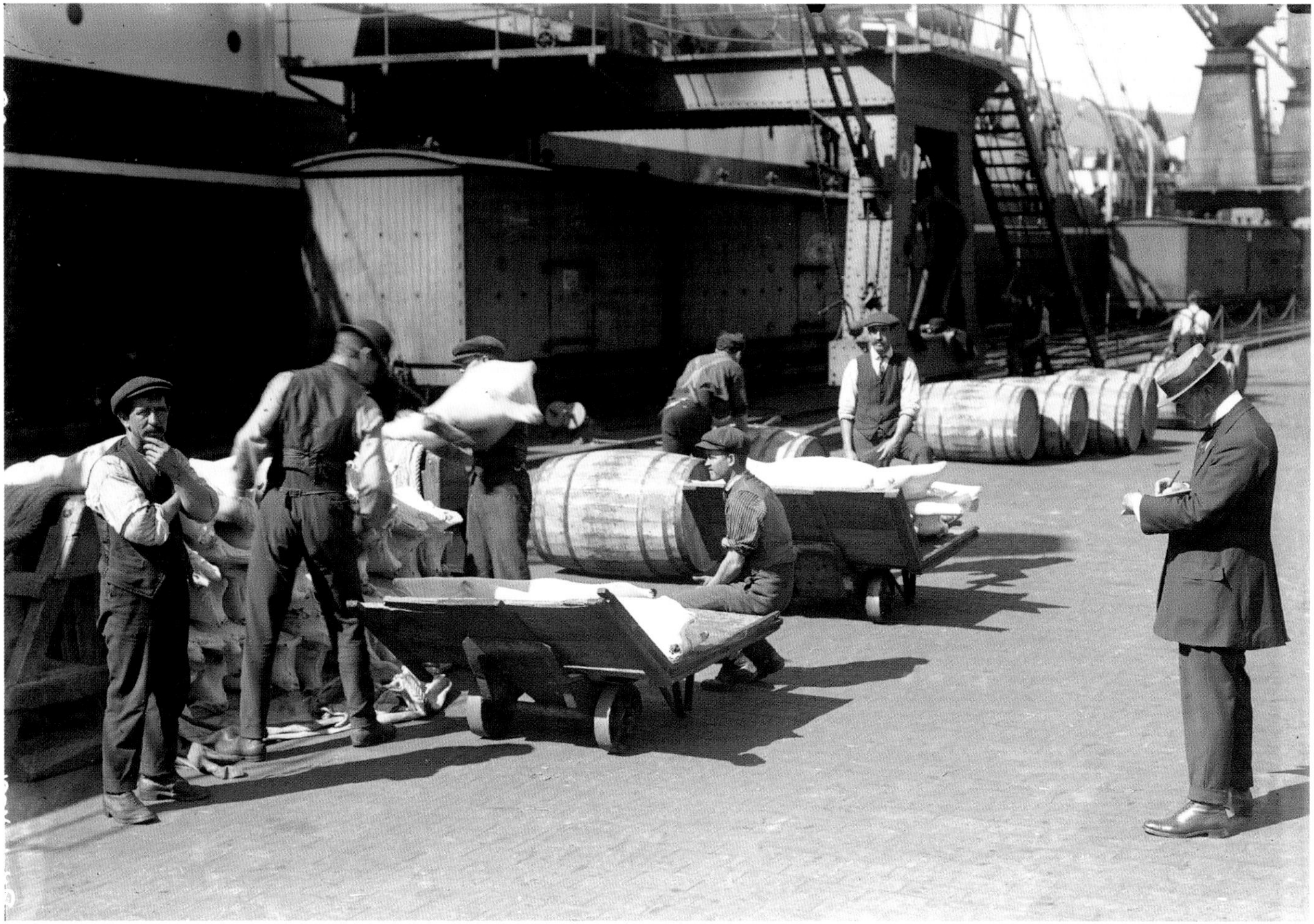

2. At the Wharves

Give us paid birthdays, double overtime, picnic holidays, and all that wine
Give us the Jubilee Dock, a ten-hour working week and, why not
Give us back the whole promenade; you've seen it there, it's lying dead

Bring in the army, Farmer Bill, it's dangerous work, a bitter pill
Bring to the table everything you've got, it won't be enough, I know that much
Bring your fighting gloves and your boxing hat and tricks of law. And stand up

Look at the Union Company, sending passengers out in cattle-scows
Look at the Union Company, holding cavern prisoners in the swill room
Now look at the banners flying red, the rights of man have been all but bled
Look at the banners flying red, the rights of man have been all but bled
Come on

Now look at the wharves chock-full with ice-cream stalls and community halls
No more stacks of wool, frozen meat palettes hauled along heavy rope slings
Just a steady stream of yellow saddle trucks coming out from the North end
There's nothing more, it's hard to bear. So it is. So it is.

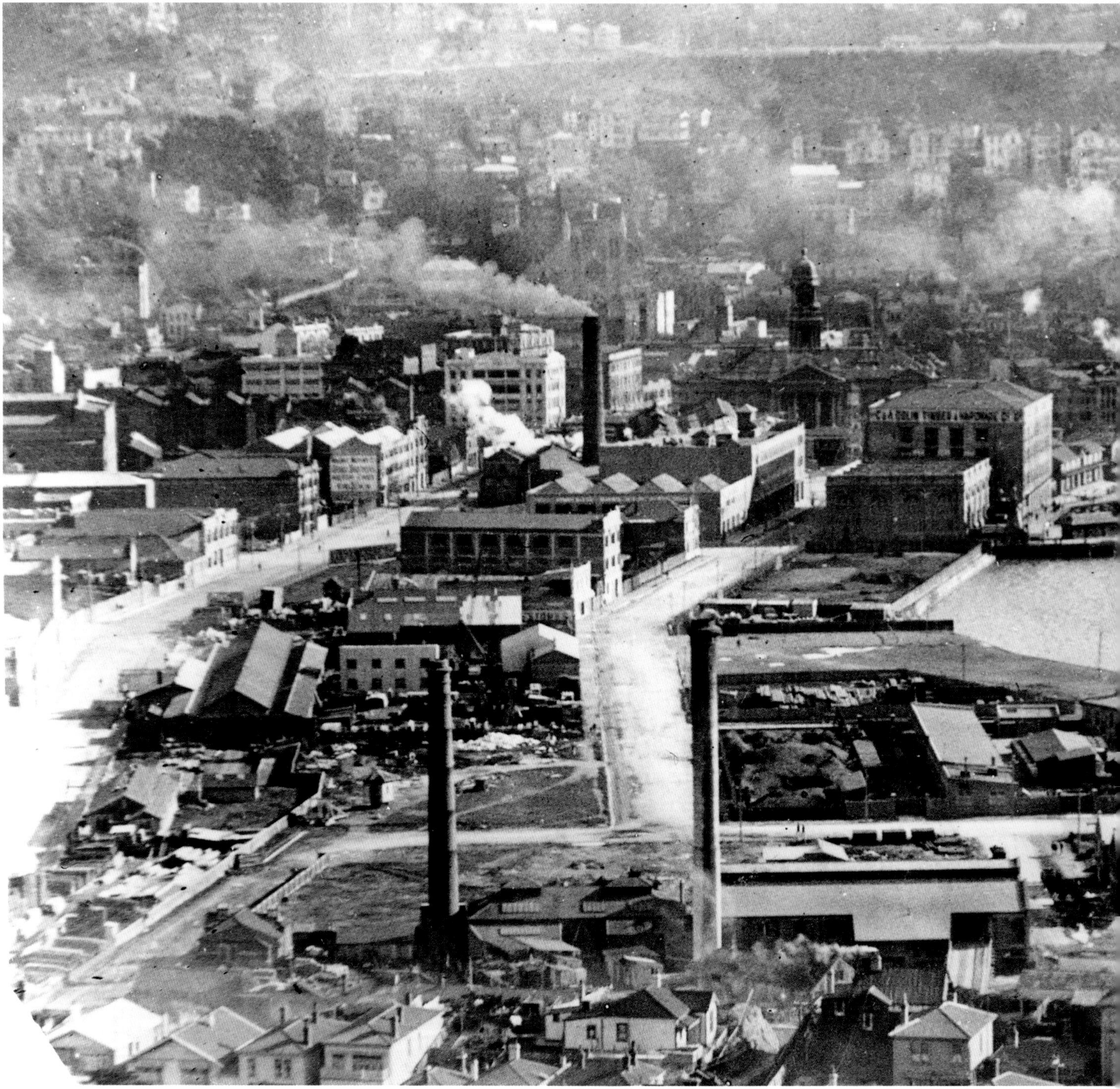

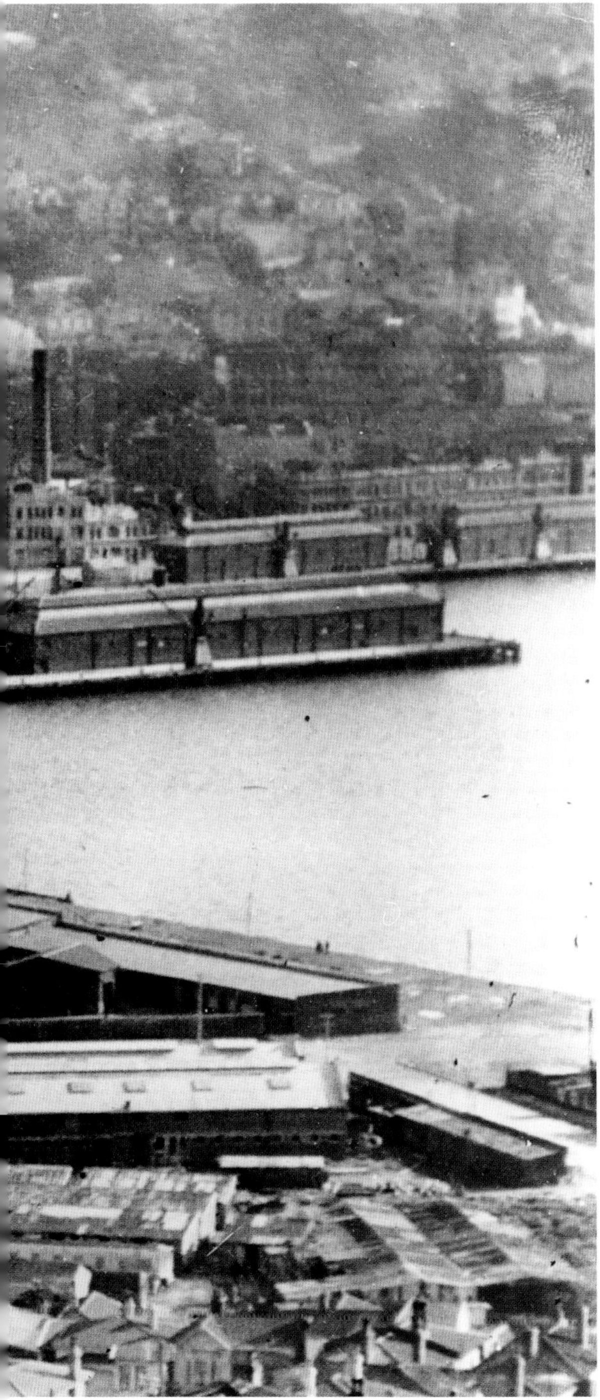

THIS IS THE TIME

The first three decades of the 20th century were cut in two by the horrors of the First World War. Few households were left untouched by death, either from the War or the influenza that followed it. But it was also a time of growth and change. The rise of commercial flight, film and jazz, the introduction of cars and coffee, and the foundation of new social movements made for an action-packed era. Much of Wellington's shape today is a legacy of these thirty years. The earth was carved and reformed to make room for new houses, streets and suburbs.

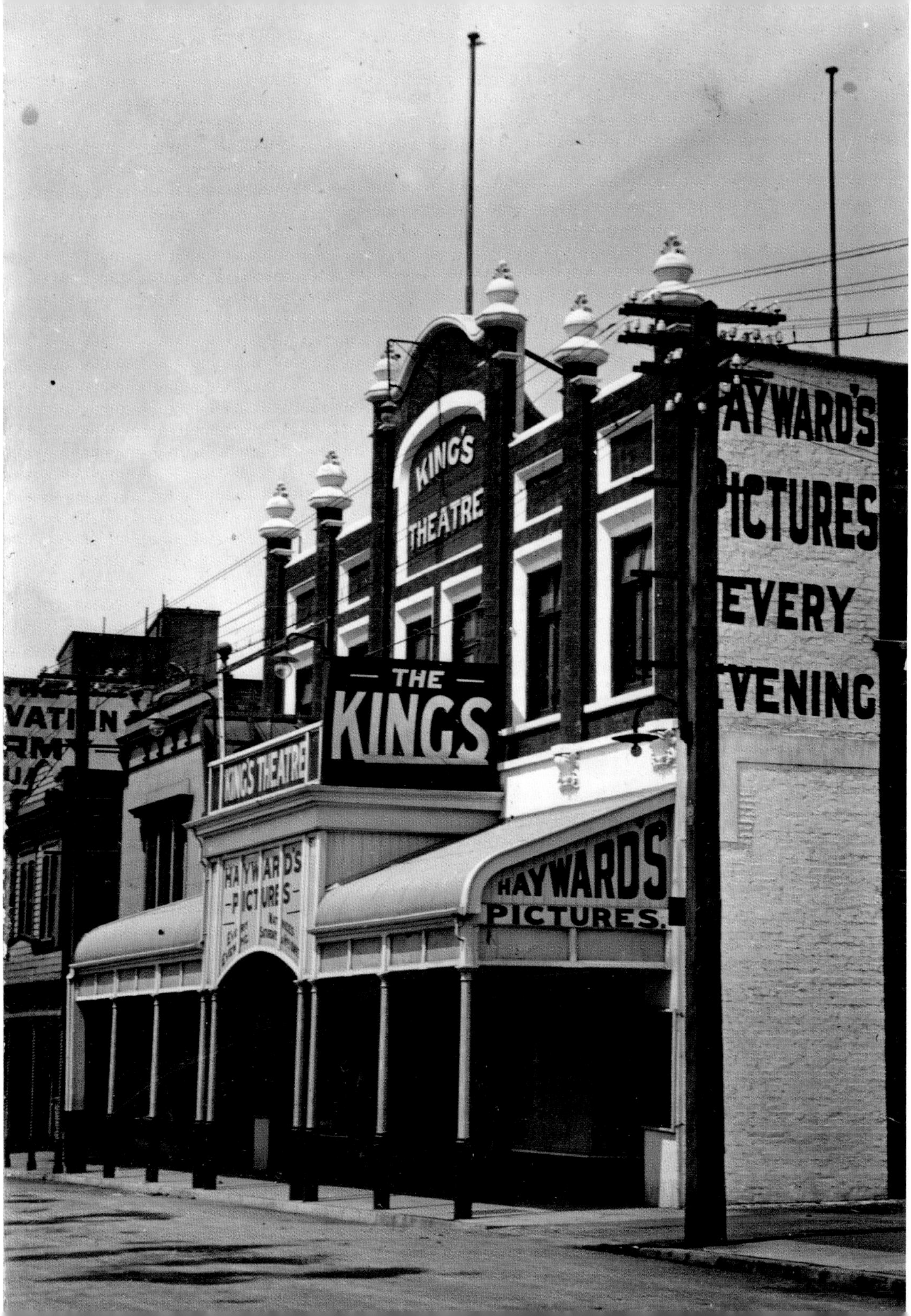
KING'S THEATRE
THE KINGS
KING'S THEATRE
HAYWARD'S PICTURES EVERY EVENING
HAYWARD'S PICTURES
HAYWARD'S PICTURES.

3. This is the Time

This is the time of the spinning wheels
And tunnels cut through the stone
That led us, that lead us to our homes

This is the time
Of isolation and opportunity
From a land rising up
With its bright new city halls

This is the time
Of lion hearts and kings
The public trust is born
To the tune of a clarinet
From the city band

This is the time, we take to the air
We take arms to the streets, dive the straits
With Pelorus Jack at our heels
While the country is at war
We intern the foreign names, settle scores
Lose ourselves in Turnbull's vast stores
This is the time, this is the time

This is the time
Of moving pictures and moral crusade
Sliding down the muddy banks
This is the time
To leave our thanks
This is the time
This is the time

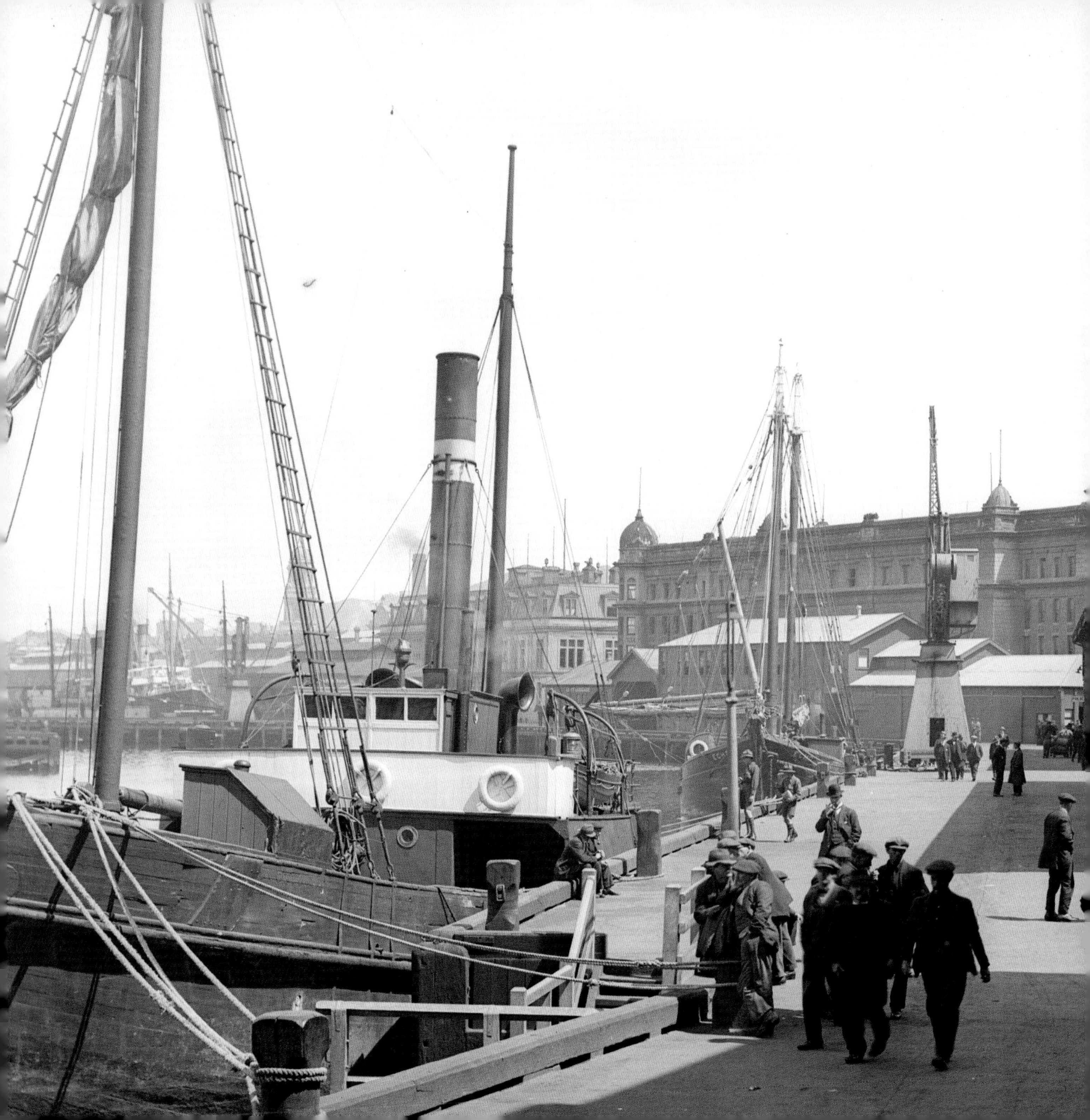

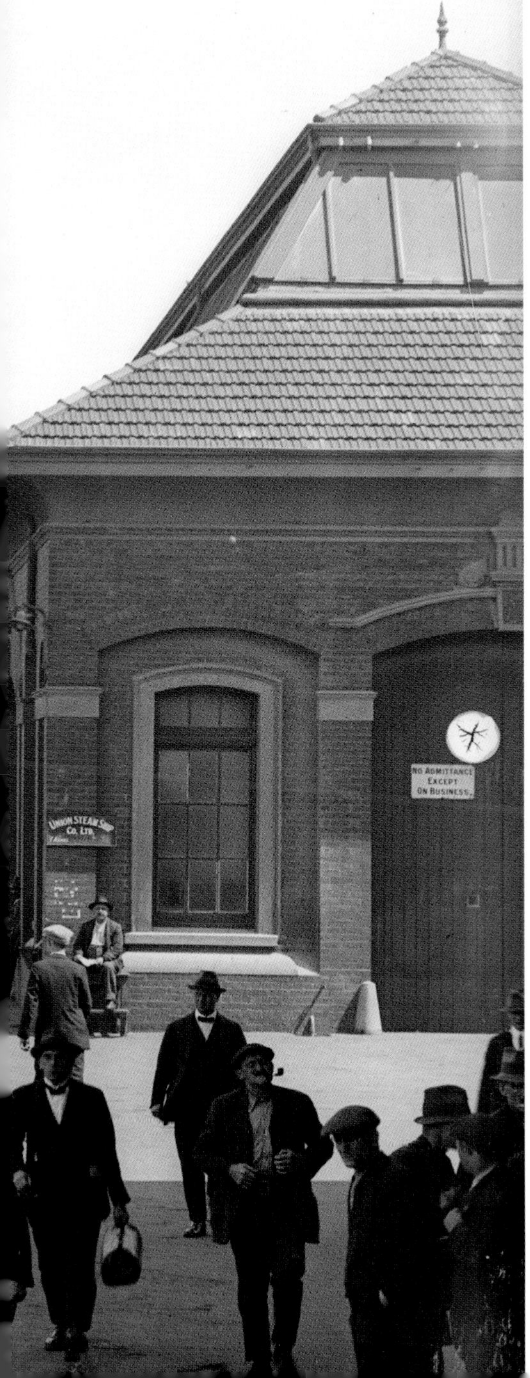

MAYOR GEORGE TROUP

In the 1930s, the Great Depression brought massive unemployment to New Zealand. Wellington suffered greatly but it fared better than many cities. Much of its success can be attributed to the mayor at the time, George Troup, who was able to put the unemployed to work by creating forward-thinking public works such as the construction of the airport. Sadly for the city, ill health prevented him from standing for a second term. Things weren't nearly so rosy for the average Wellingtonian after he retired from office, as the Government proceeded to take advantage of the willing workforce that Troup had inspired, making working conditions almost unbearable.

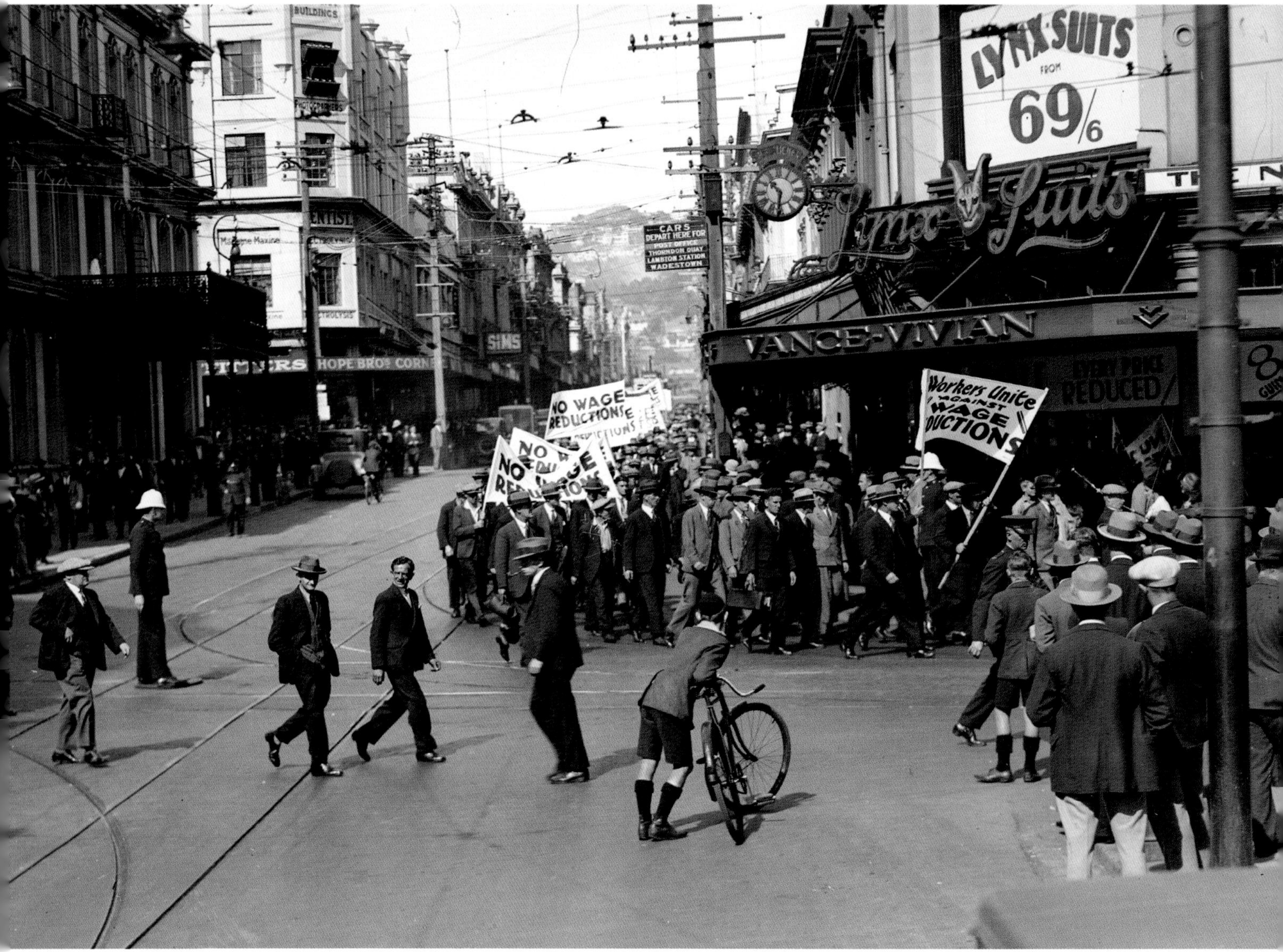
LYNX SUITS
FROM
69/6
Lynx Suits
VANCE-VIVIAN
CARS
DEPART HERE FOR
POST OFFICE
THORNDON QUAY
LAMBTON STATION
WADESTOWN
NO WAGE
REDUCTIONS
Workers Unite
AGAINST
WAGE
DUCTIONS
EVERY PRICE
REDUCED
SIMS
HOPE BROS CORNE
BUILDINGS
Madame Maxine

4. Mayor George Troup

What started out from the seeds of the empire
The golden path would start to turn and tire
The golden path that could never ever fail
Begins to take a deep and dark trail
While the trail for some will still climb higher
There's a sense that most are sinking further

Mayor George Troup, he stood up and said 'Surely we
can do something', this city ain't dead
Tunnels go through the mud rock soil
The lucky ones get to scrape and toil
Further was the message from the Ministry
Shades of Marie Antoinette, there's nothing to believe in
Out on the ground, nobody was sitting quiet
Down the town was the cry – a full-blood riot

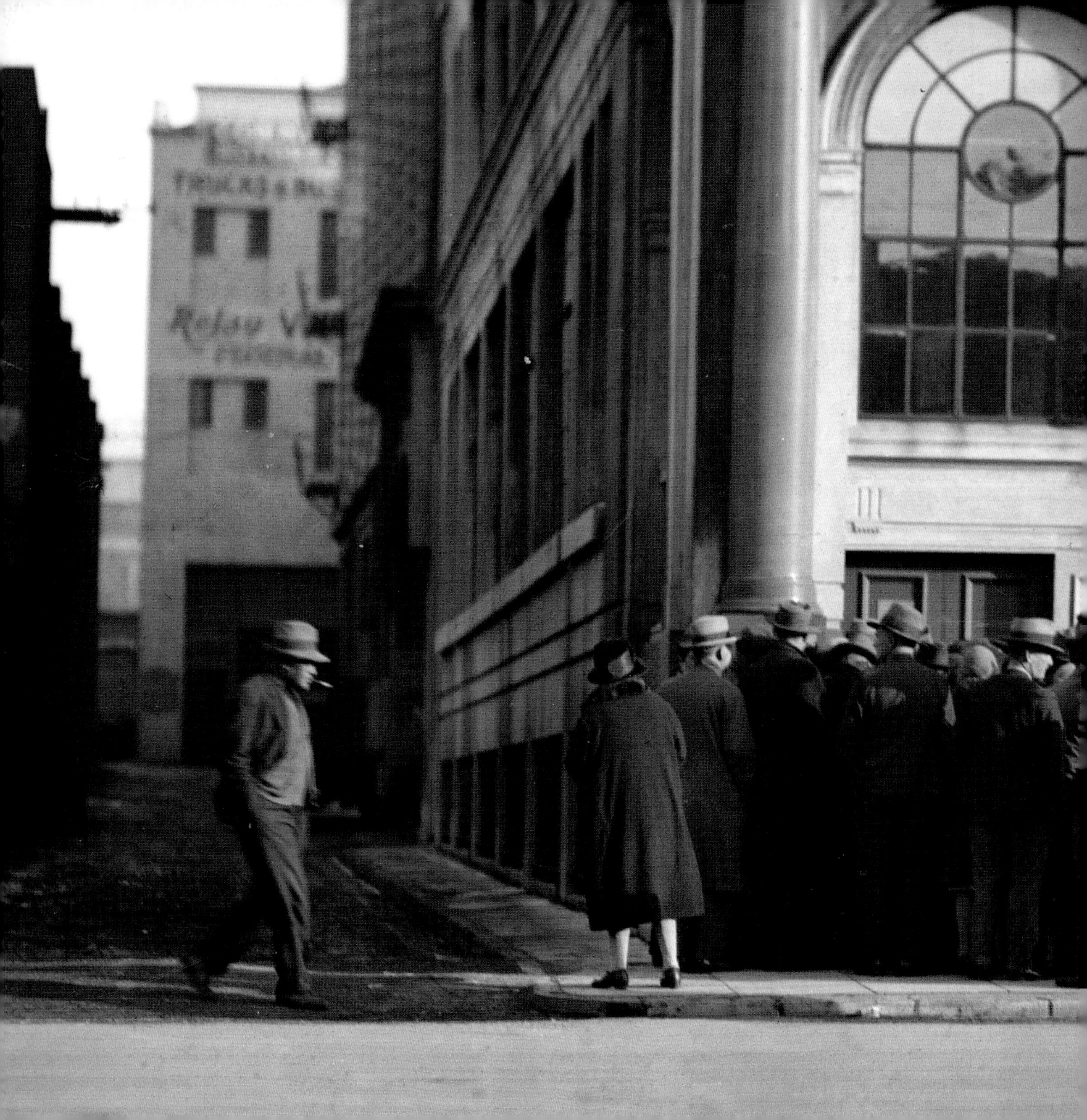

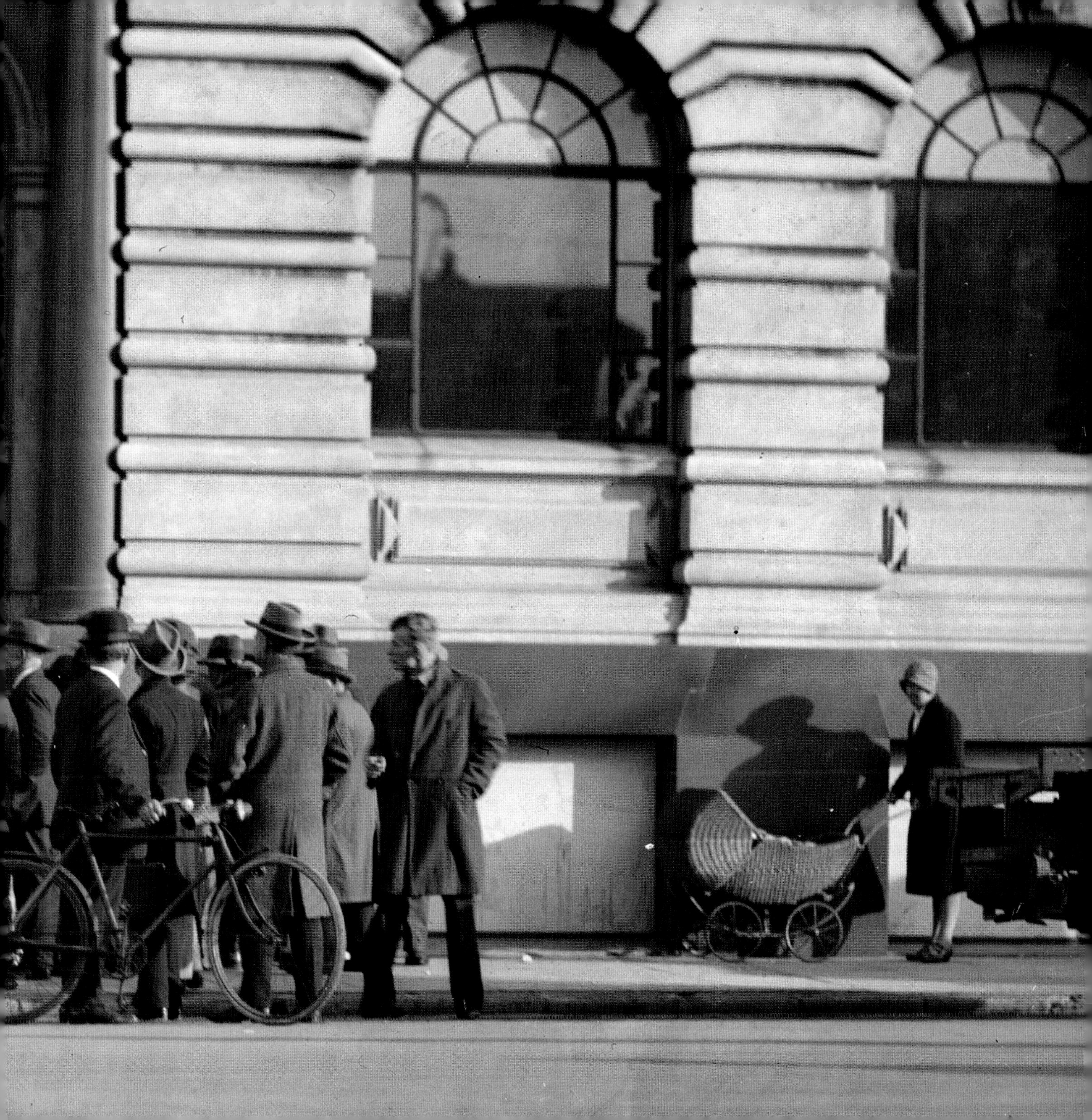

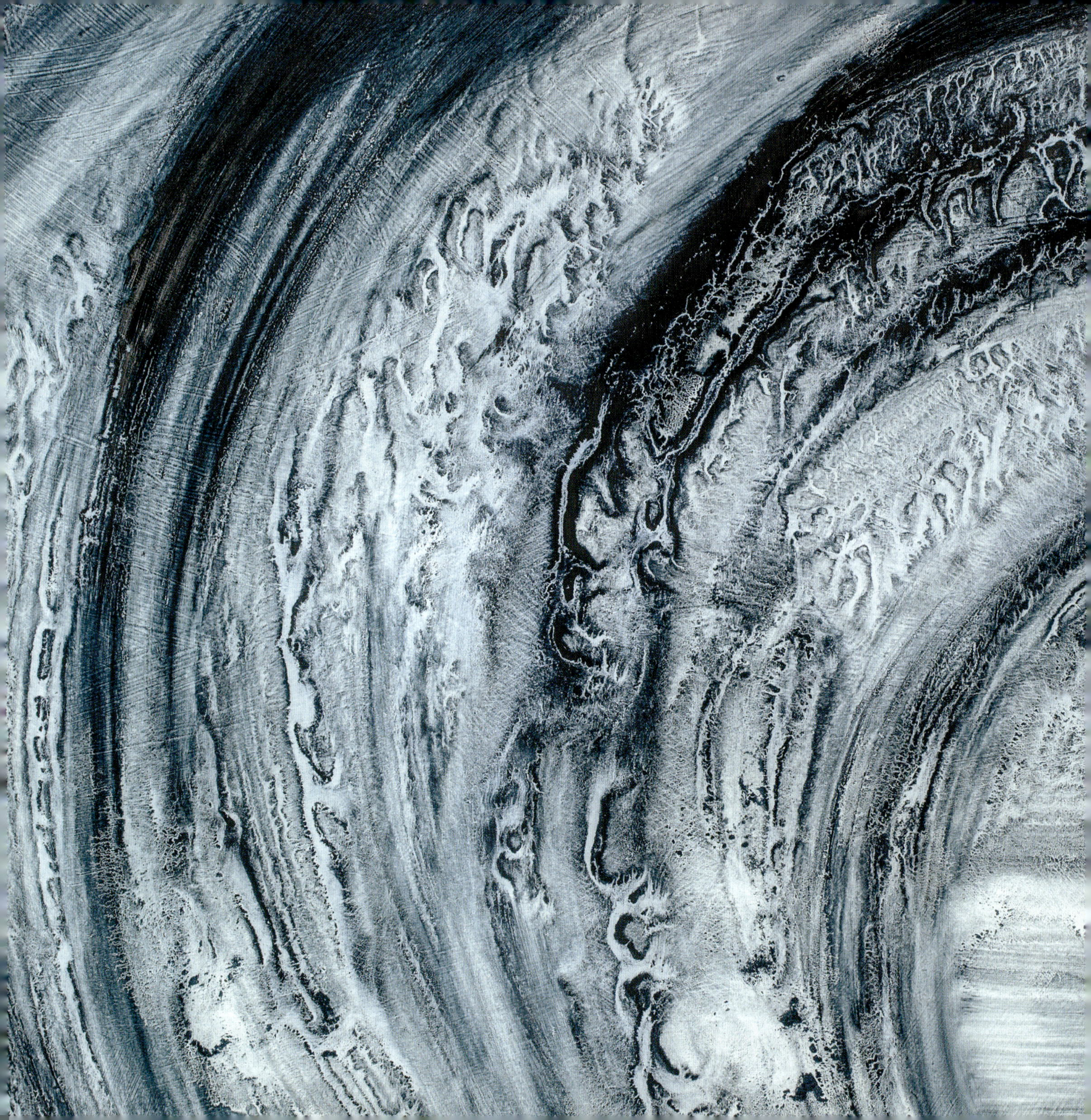

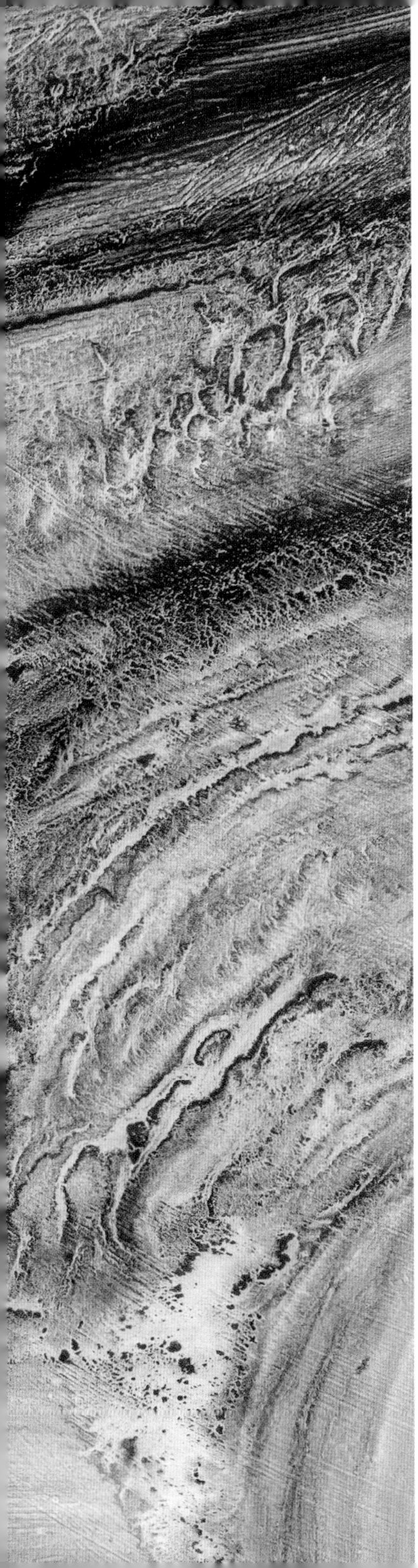

AFTER THE WAR

The Second World War was followed by another period of economic gain in the 1950s. It was a conservative time for good, grey New Zealand: people had a strong desire for stability after thirty years of radically changing fortunes. Wellingtonians were happy with the status quo. However, these good times were in some ways a smokescreen, as there remained a number of unresolved social issues, such as income inequality, poor workers' rights and ongoing injustices towards Māori. During the 1960s and 70s, increasing pressure finally began to bring about much-needed social reforms. In this period, Wellington artists and writers flourished, and a number gained national acclaim.

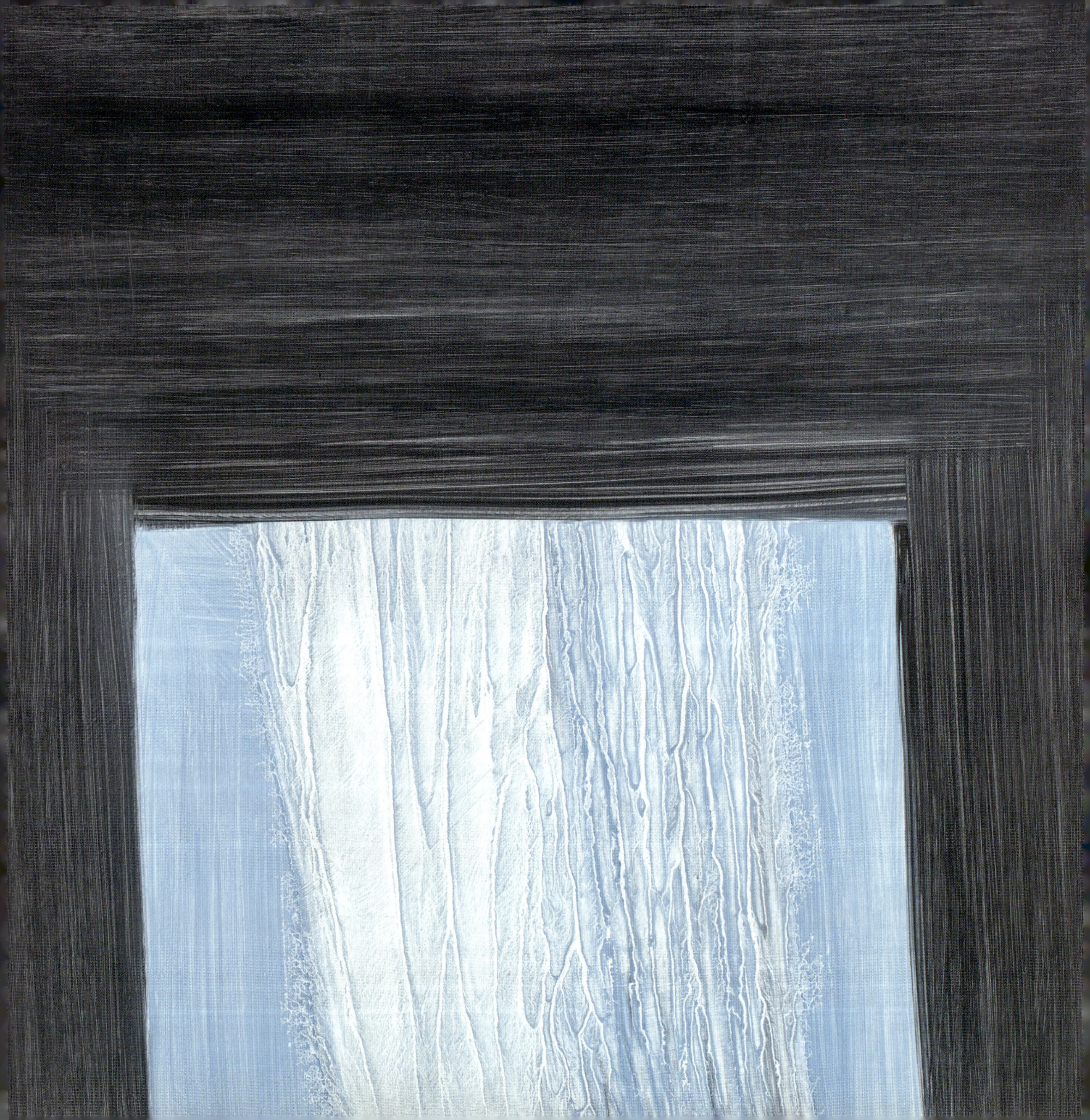

5. After the War

They say that after the war we
Gave up courage in store and
Found our way downstream
Found our way

Tore up the tram tracks
Gave us the welfare state
Hid from the unarmed truth this
Would only lead to dissent

The year of the monkey and
Broken-down barricades we
Take course to liberate all
Things under the sun

Call out the alienators
From the seaside cafes
Do not walk dully home
Let the Māori Jesus free

Turns out we don't even know
Believe all that we are shown
Throw out the prescription so
Stay put, take what you want

Forget about the past
Follow the well-worn path
Go on, just smile and wave
Everybody loves you but yourself

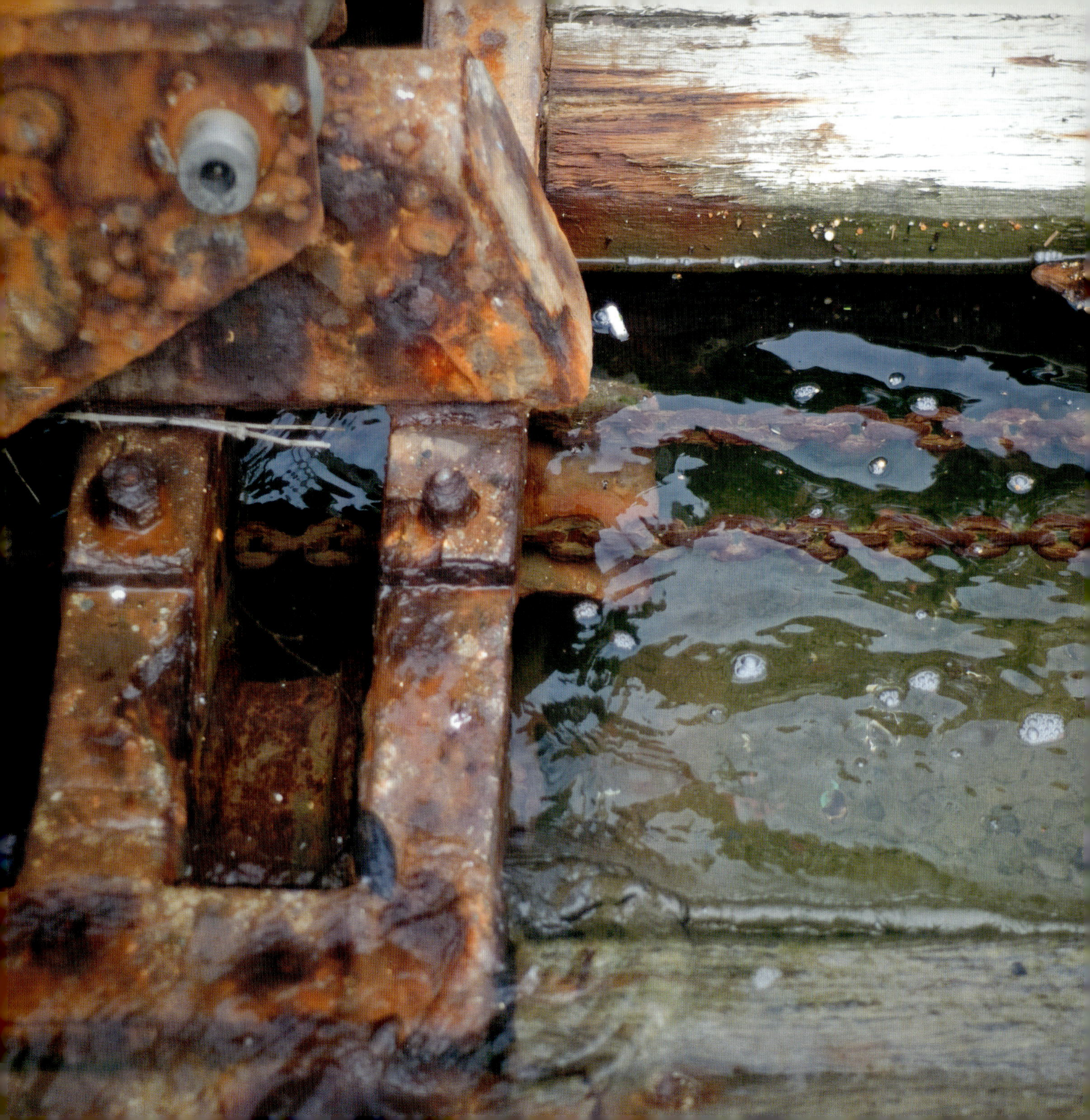

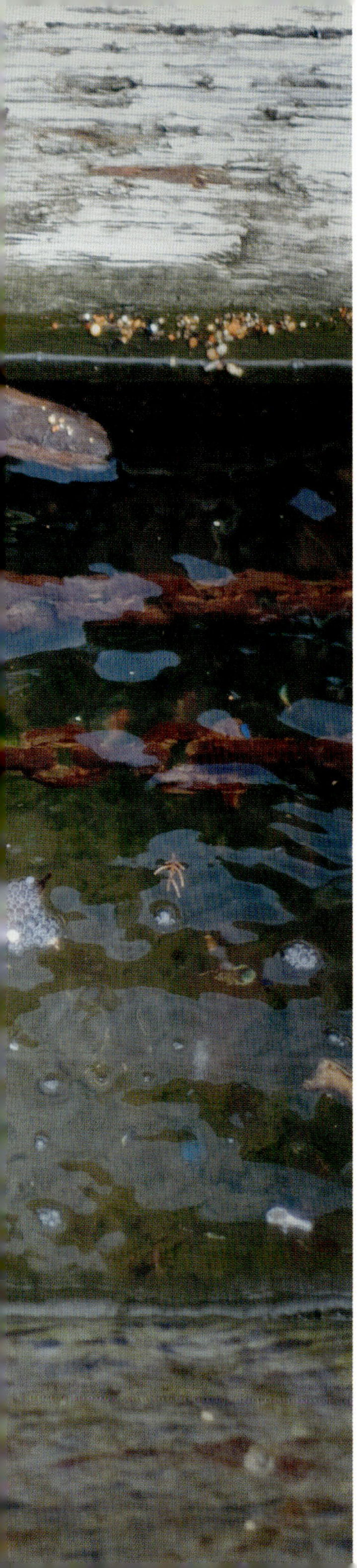

SHIP SONG

The Port of Wellington has seen a huge number of ships pass through its heads. While there have been a few famous ones, the collective stories of the smaller, less important vessels are equally compelling. They read like characters from a novel or soap opera, living long, complicated and colourful lives. Much like the sailors who shipped out on them, their lives inevitably ran their course. Some went to breakers' yards, but many are wrecks on Wellington's wild coast or at the bottom of the harbour.

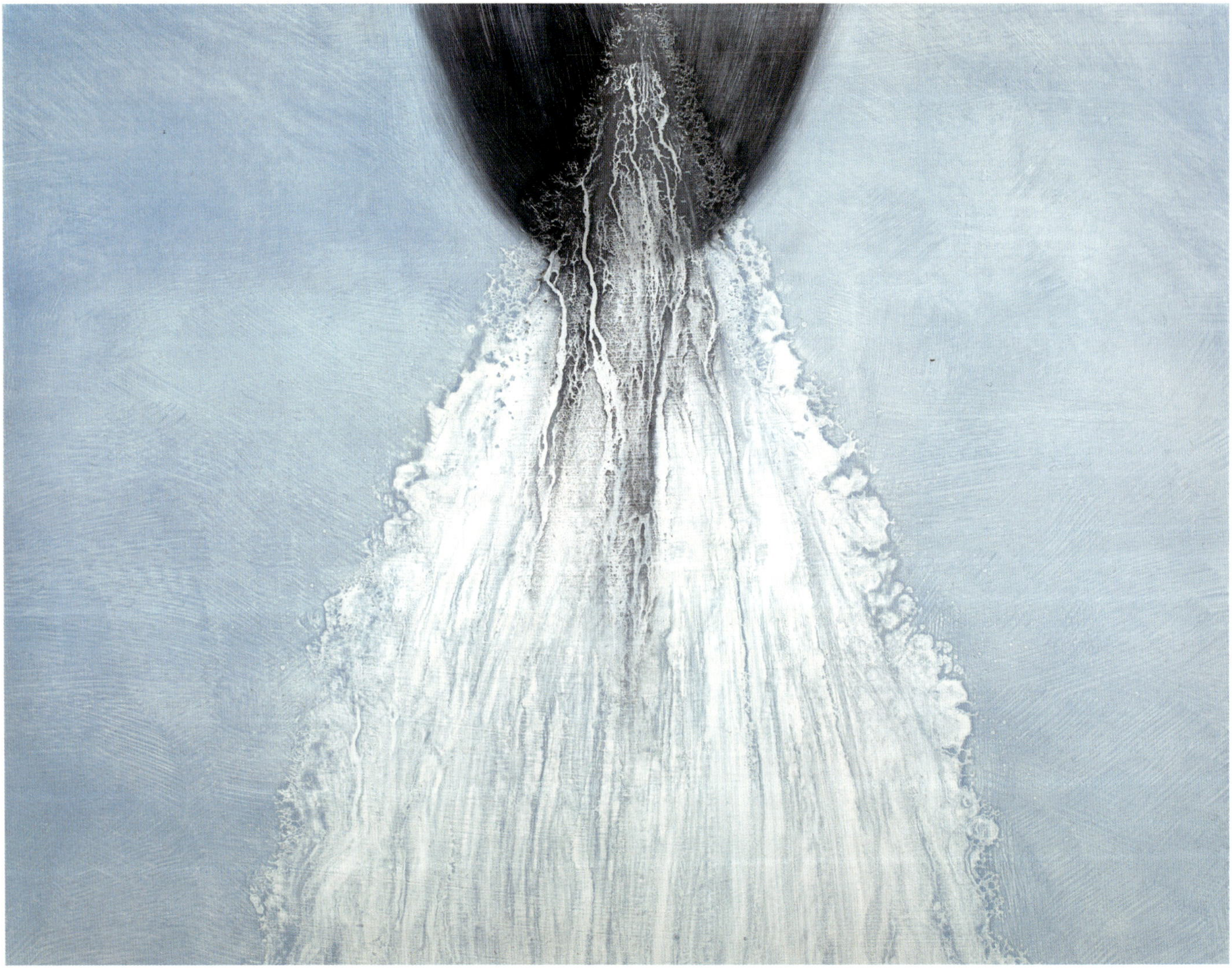

6. Ship Song

The Maimai was a sleepy tub
She could barely turn around
She was solid gold tenfold
Though she was no greyhound

There was a sister ship, the South Sea
She had the conning of an admiral's fleet
She was a crazed thing, a rare packet
She had a mood for every petal on a flower

Now they're both lying together
In the bottom of the same harbour
  down there below
Now they're both lying forever
By the good old-time canteen
  down in Fiddler's Green.

The rusted hulls and layered paint
Twisted ropes swinging above board
It's not *The Leaving of Liverpool*
Something more wonderful

And what of corncob pipes
Lit up when the southerly bites
Overturned and overwhelmed
You wonder why they ever left port

What of Jock Cardnough?
All the names on brass plaques hung
On those teak-stained walls
Well they're all lying together
In the bottom of the same harbour
  down there below
I guess they're all lying forever
By the good old-time canteen
Down in Fiddler's Green
  down there below.

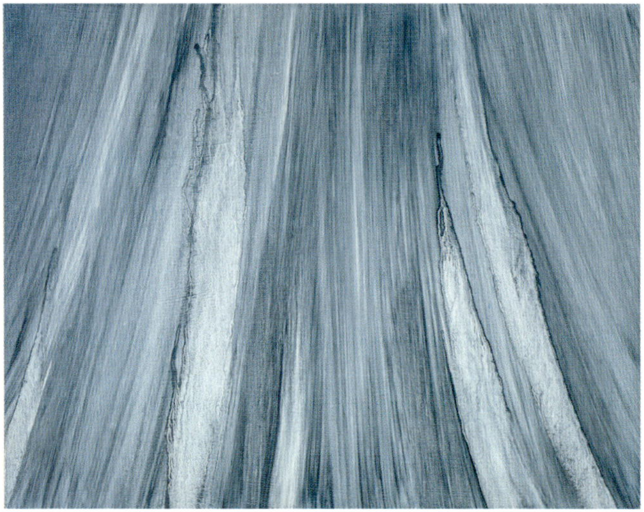
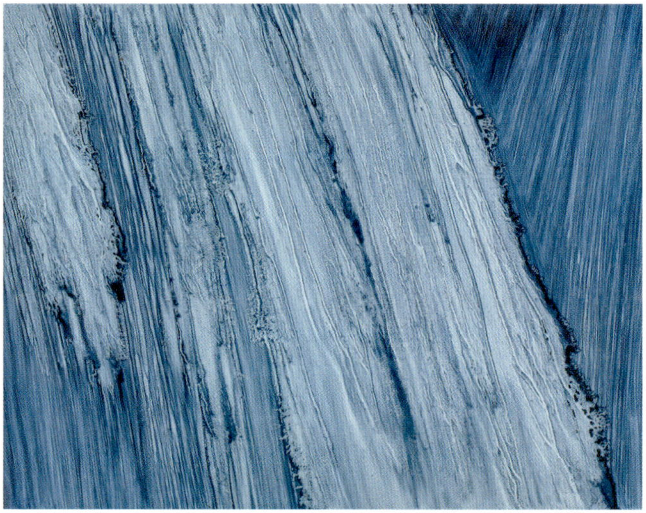
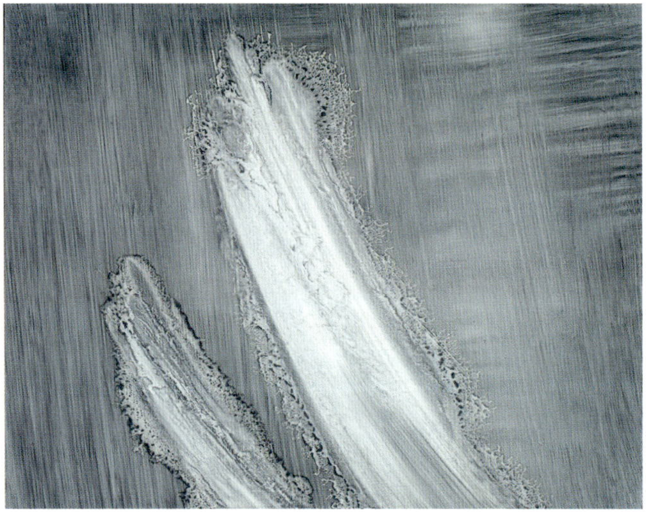
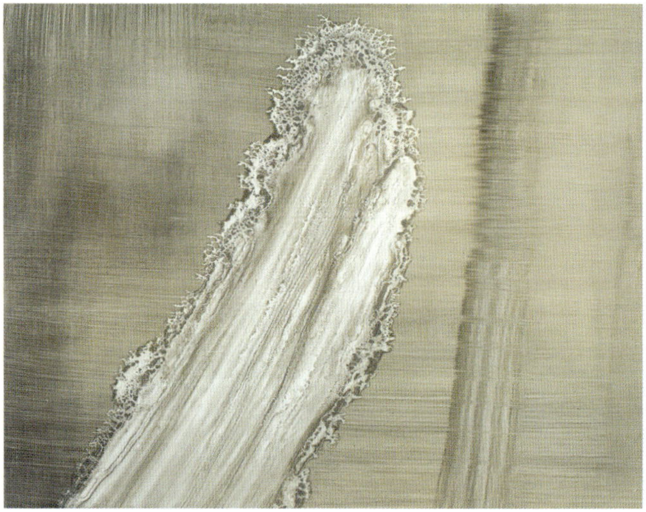

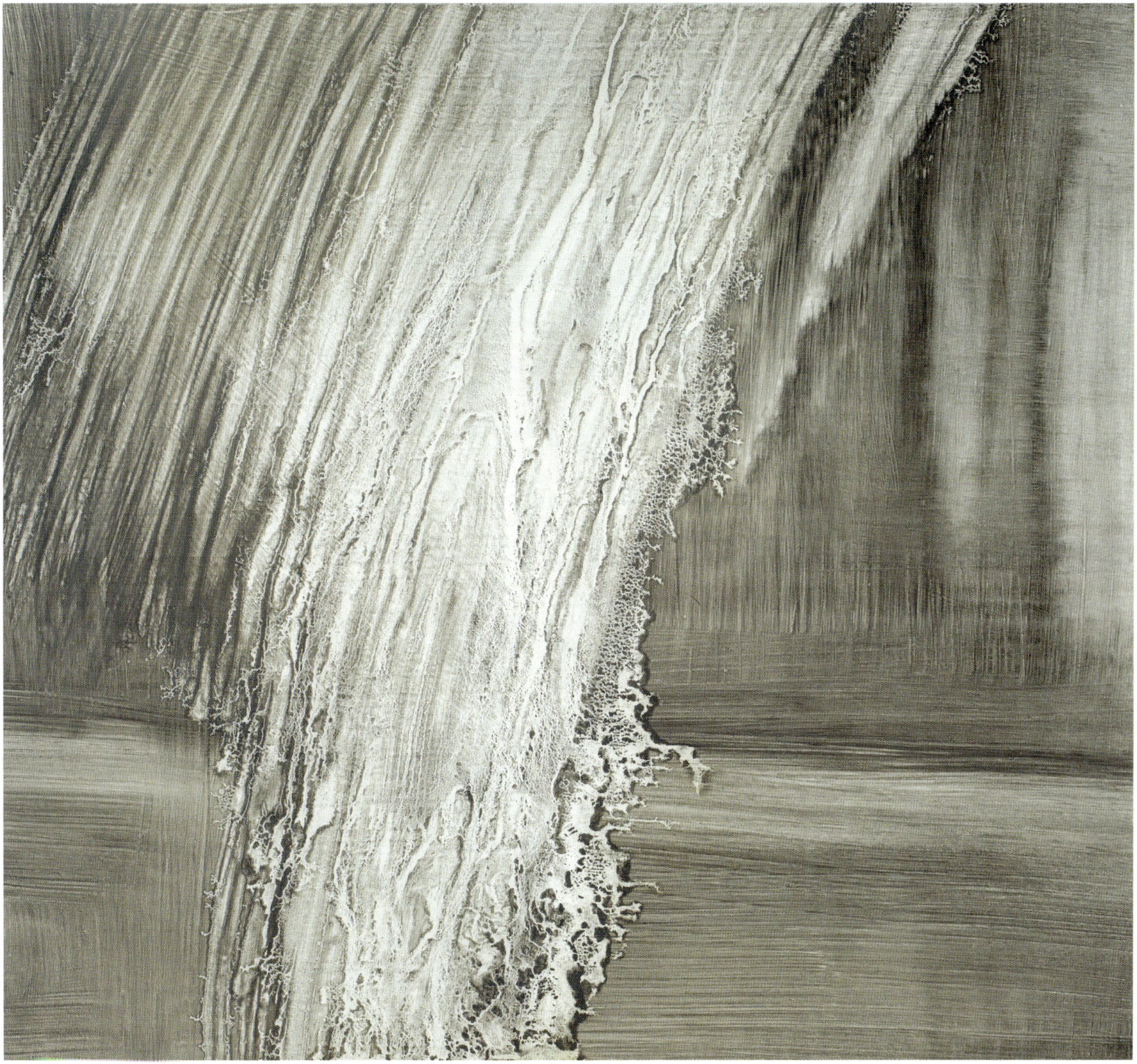

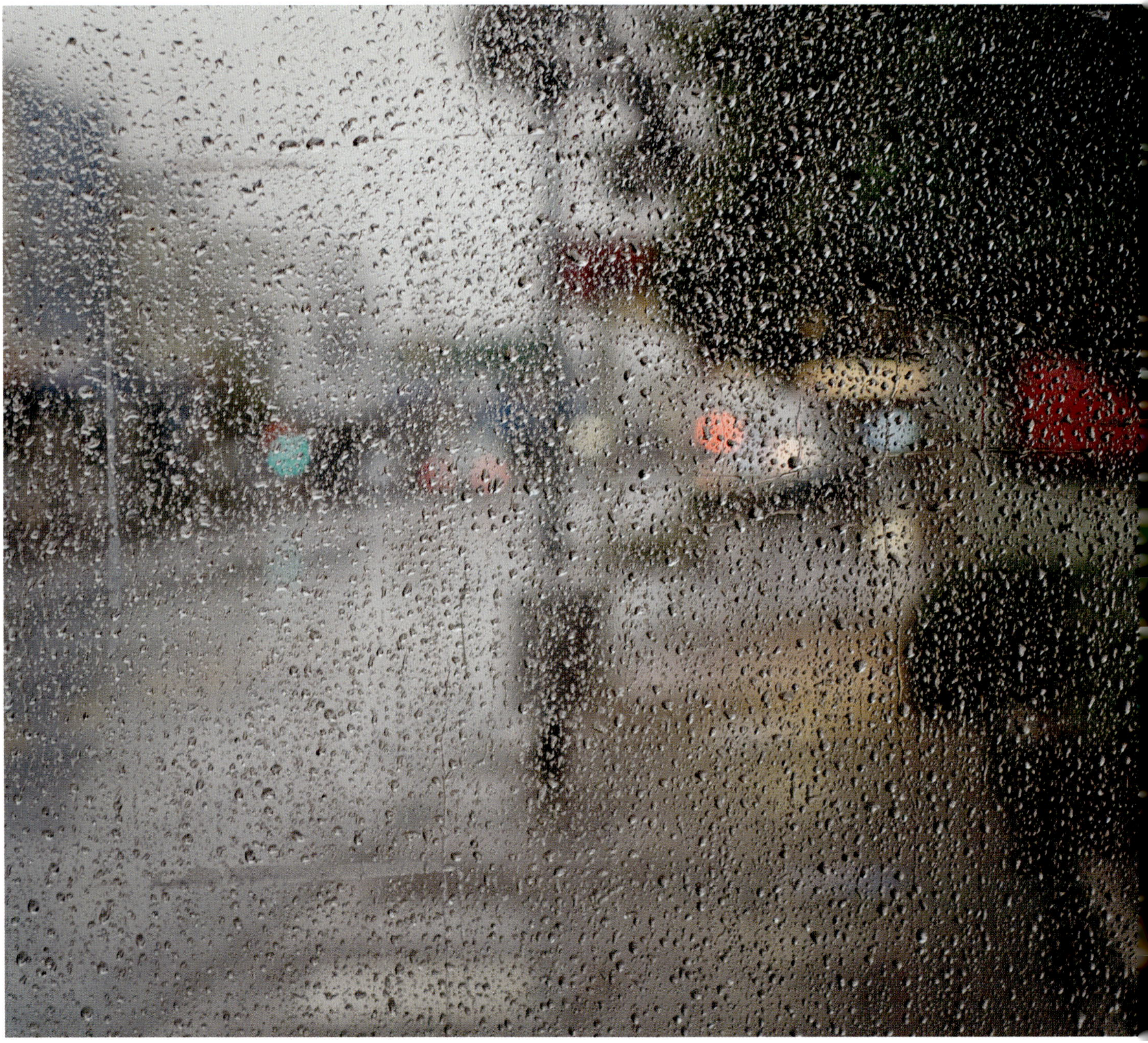

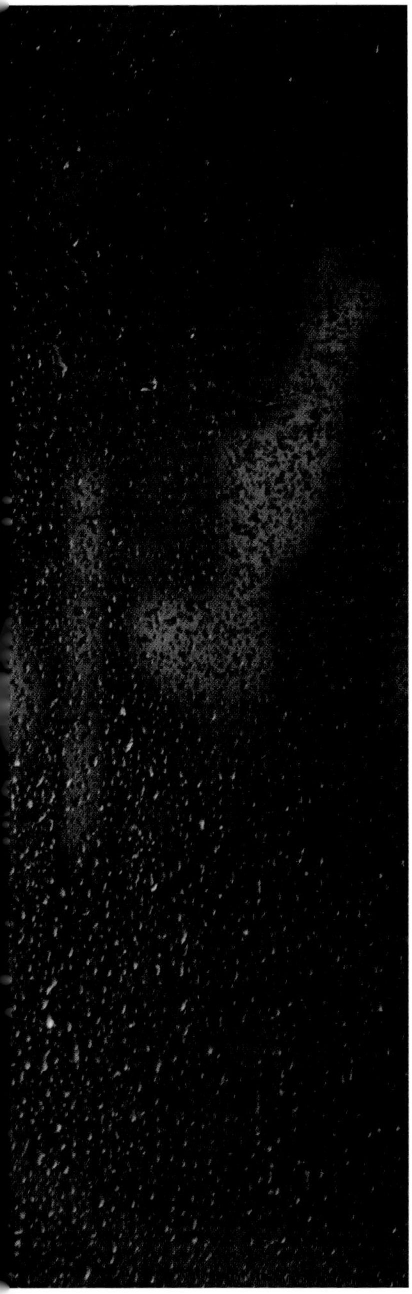

RED STANDS FOR THE *CUBA*

The *Cuba* was one of the first immigrant ships to arrive in New Zealand. After its arrival in 1840, town planners named Cuba Street after the ship. It ran in a direct line to the wharves and the harbour. This connection between immigration, the city and sea was cut in the 1980s by the construction of the Michael Fowler Centre, which blocked the view entirely. With the nautical connection gone, the street has forged an identity with the country that gave its name to the ship. Red stands for Cuba: the ship, the country and also, of course, the street's fountain with its multicoloured buckets endlessly cycling water.

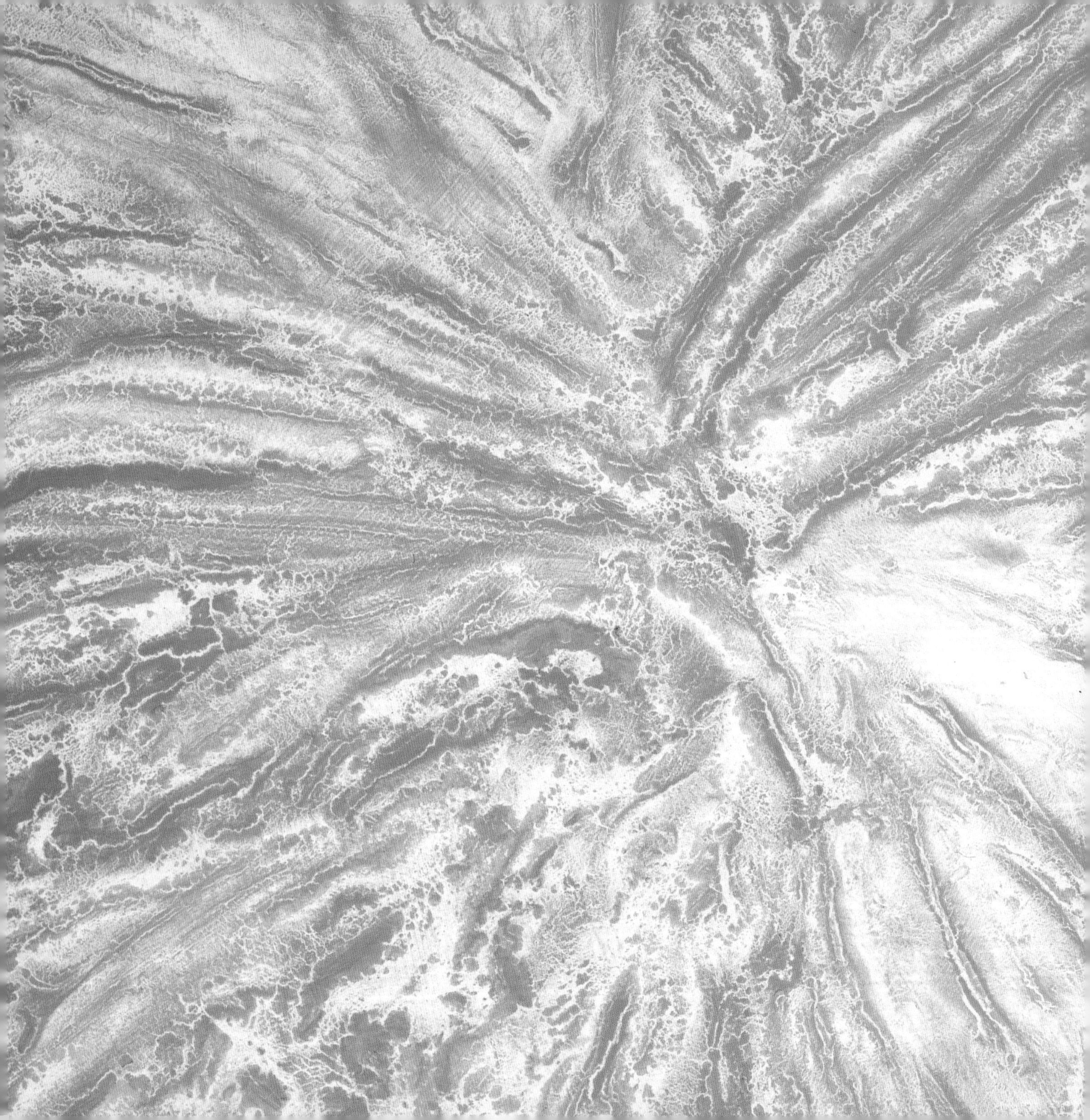

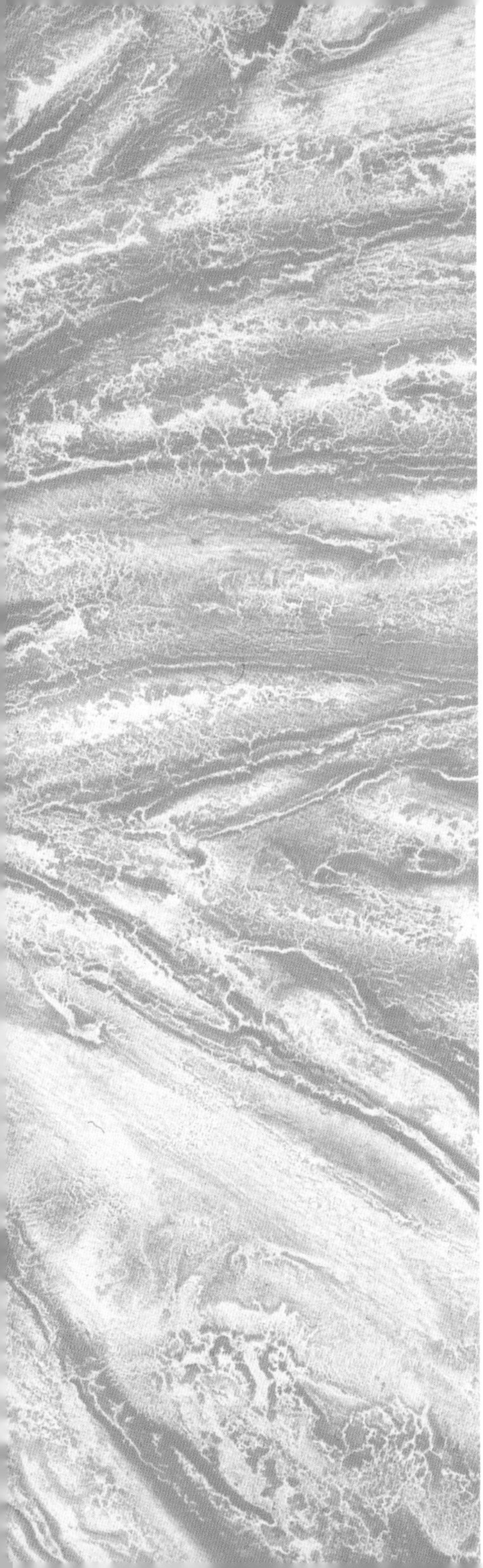

7. Red Stands for the *Cuba*

Red falls to yellow then to orange down to blue
Red tips for the *Cuba*, for the blood in me and you
Yellow is off-centre, it spills to the street
Orange stands before the sea that we came in on
Blue is where everything must run to, even that will fall

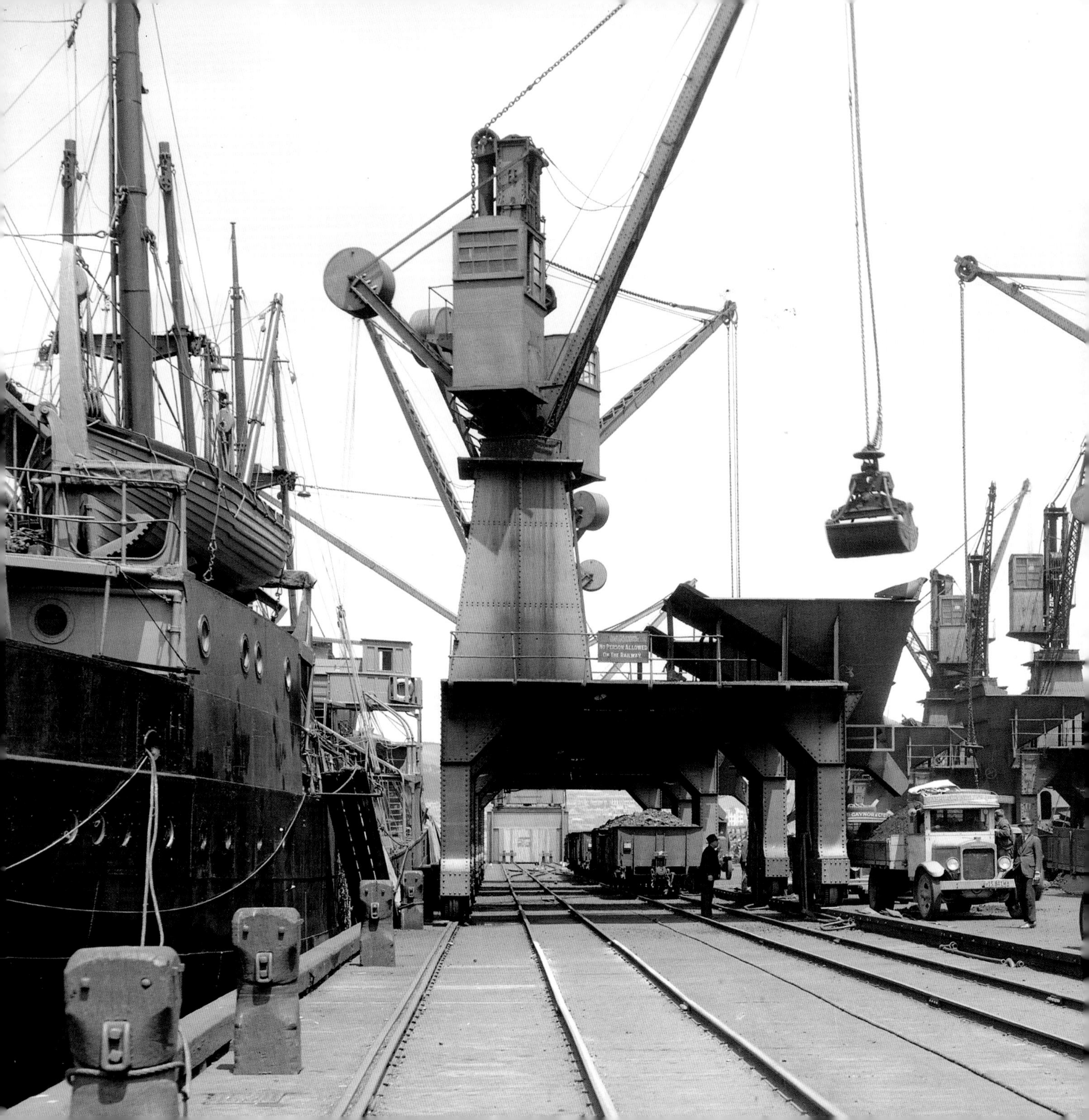
NO PERSON ALLOWED
ON THE RAILWAY

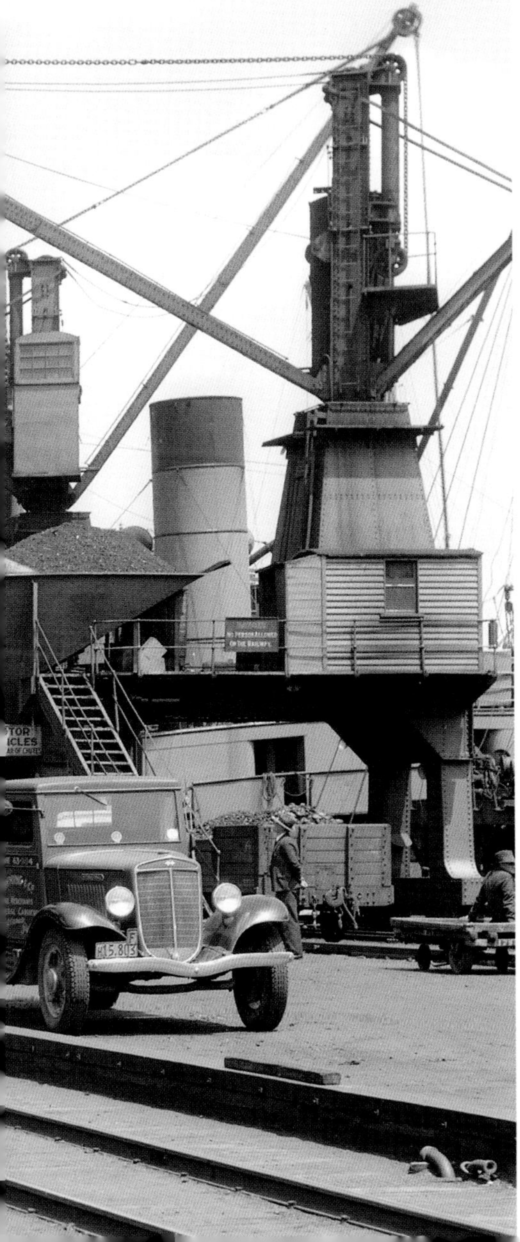

PORT OF WELLINGTON

The Port of Wellington ticked over for many years under the control of the Wellington City Corporation until William Levin persuaded the city to hand it over to the publicly elected Wellington Harbour Board in 1880. When William Jackson later added Queens Wharf to the new Board the port began to take off. It was spearheaded by a series of highly capable, business-minded chairmen who shared a passion for the success of the city, turning it at one stage into the country's largest port.

8. Port of Wellington

William Levin, well he wrested control of the harbour from the city corporation
William Jackson, he took the Queen's wharf from the city that he loved so well
Now Thomas Wilford stood for the good, he was not the lion or the fox
And Harold Beauchamp was the worst of the lot, or so said his daughter Katherine

William Cable came from over the border, a metal-working engineer by trade
And Joseph Harkness was a prohibitionist, I sure hope he wasn't like that at sea!
I saw ten thousand ships loaded with goods, sail to the motherland
Fifty thousand tonnes of the finest strong wool, half a million tonnes of coal

John McEwan was a foreman and mayor, he never put a foot wrong
And Charles Norwood was a rock who gave his lot for thirty good years
I saw a thousand hectares of old growth hardwood cut from the land we love so well
Thirty thousand sacks of pollard and sharps, that's a lot of pigs to feed

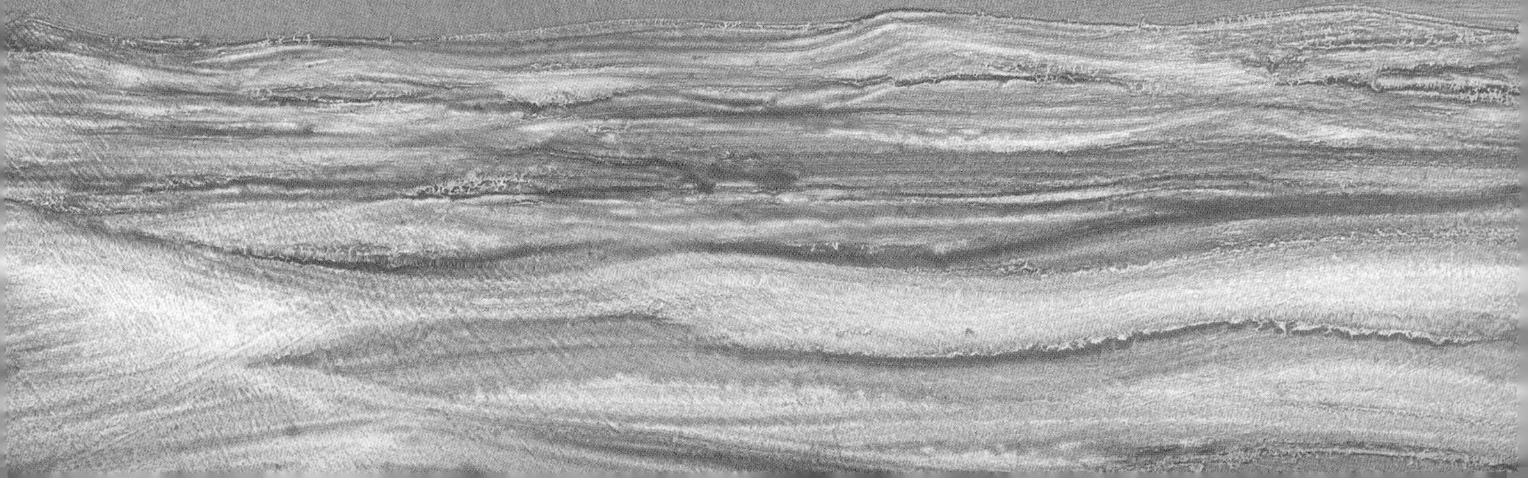

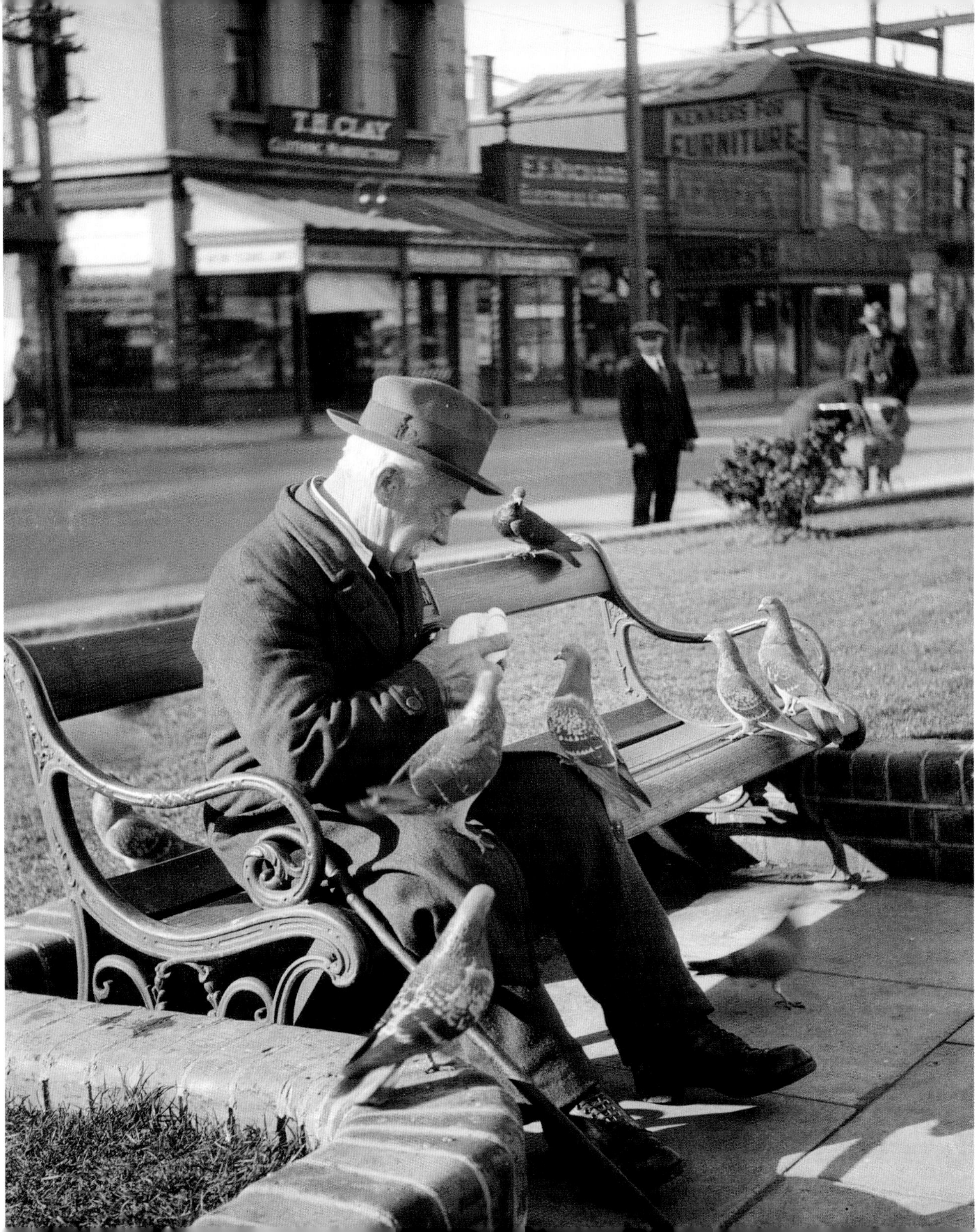
T.H.CLAY
FURNITURE

WIDE OPEN STREET

During the 1980s, partly due to concerns about damage from earthquakes, it became popular and profitable to demolish old buildings – even those that were of significant historical value. A combination of pressure from the Historic Places Trust, lobby groups and the 1987 financial crisis eventually put a halt to these proceedings. The Town Hall and a number of other wonderful buildings survived, but others, such as the impressive Spanish Mission-style Midland Hotel, weren't so lucky.

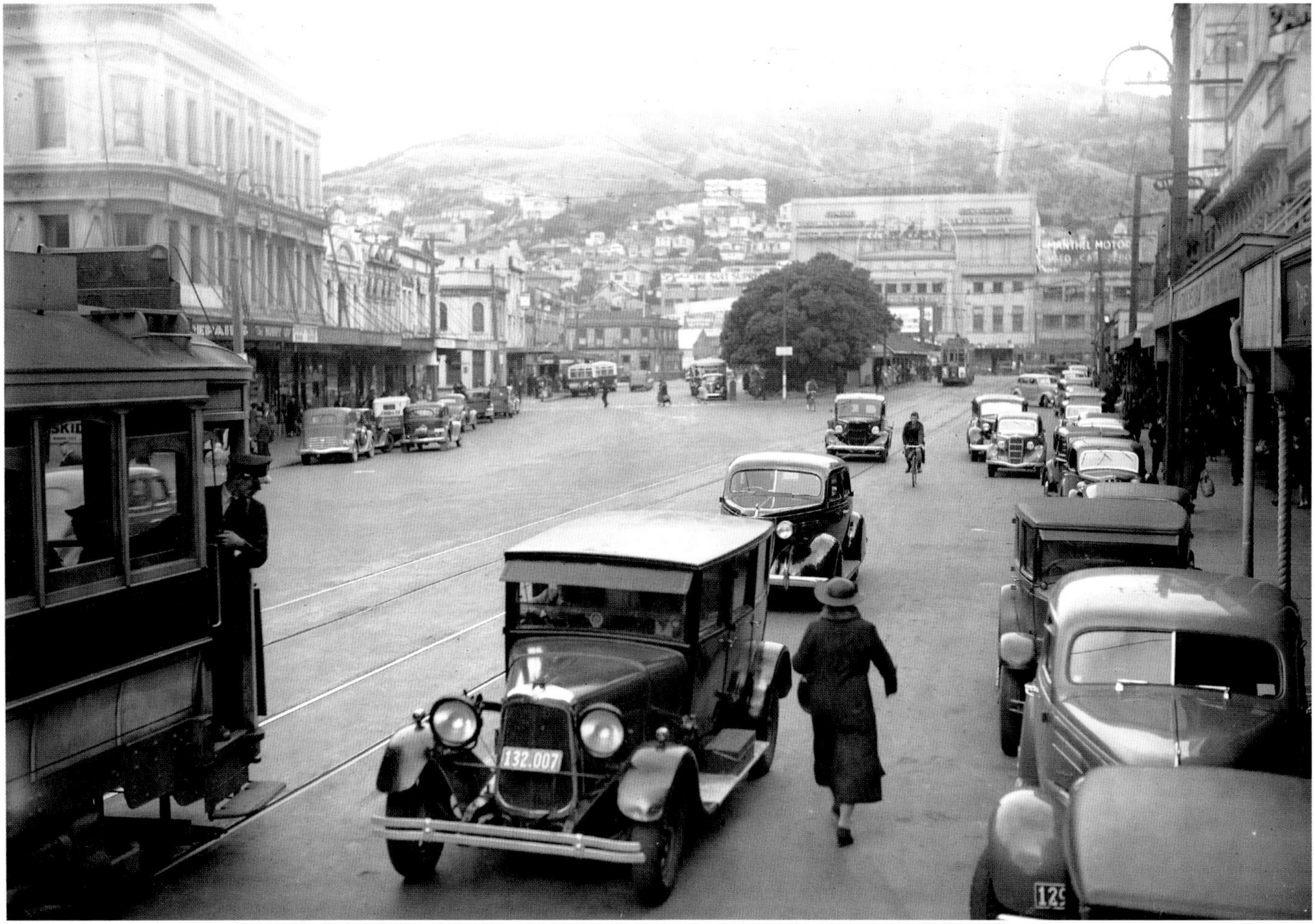
132.007

9. Wide Open Street

We stood on our wide open street
Watching over the way to the top
Gave up the Midland
The Hunter Exchange
Still wanted more

Sure it was supposed to rise
Sure it was not supposed to go

We stood on one foot then the other
Always being on the edge
We were willing to go any way

Sure it was supposed to rise
Sure it was not supposed to go

Hang your coat in the city
Hang it where you like
Who turned around to face
Who gave up the chase

Sure it was supposed to rise
Sure it was not supposed to go
Sure it was supposed to rise
Sure it was not supposed to go

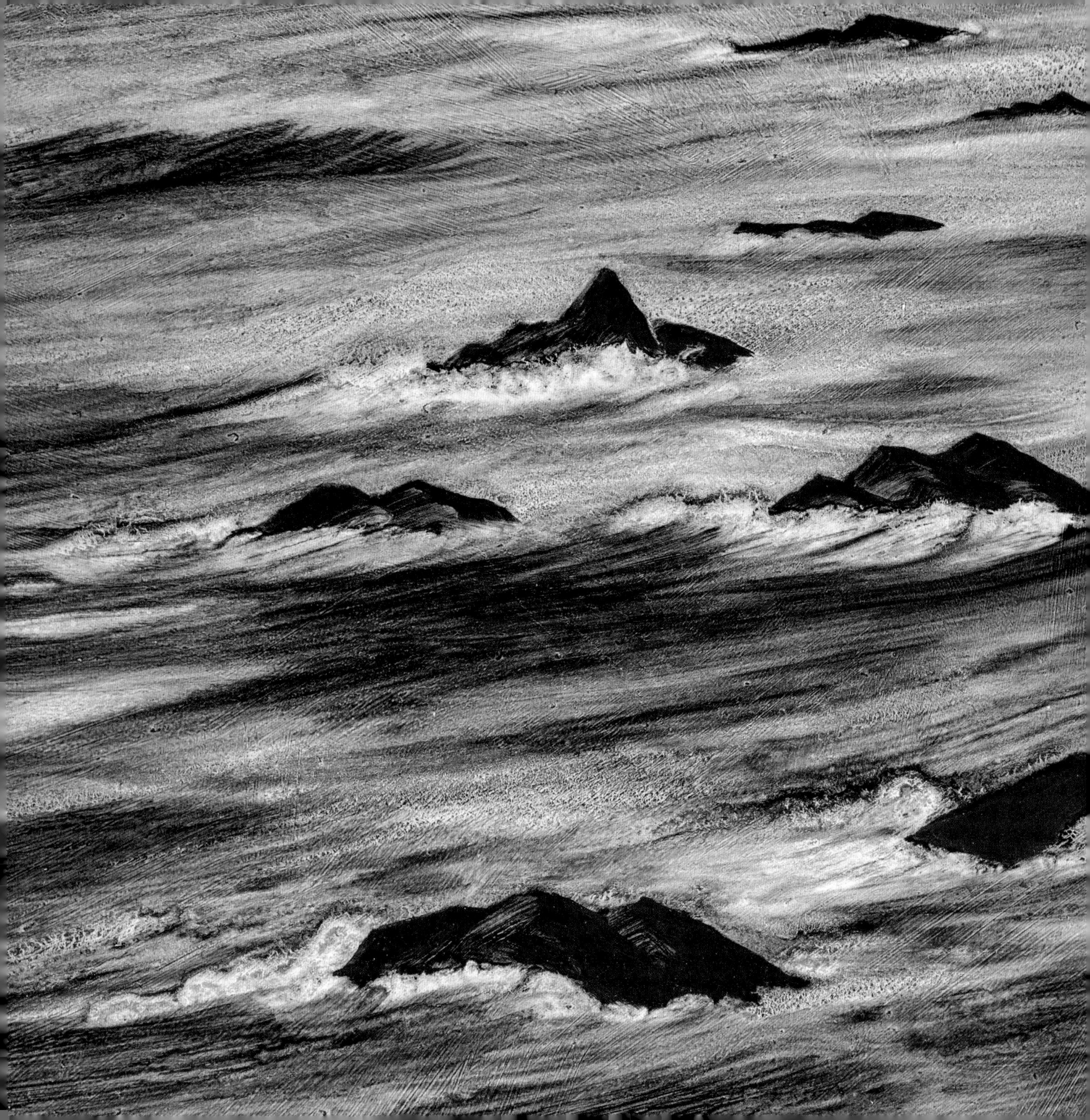

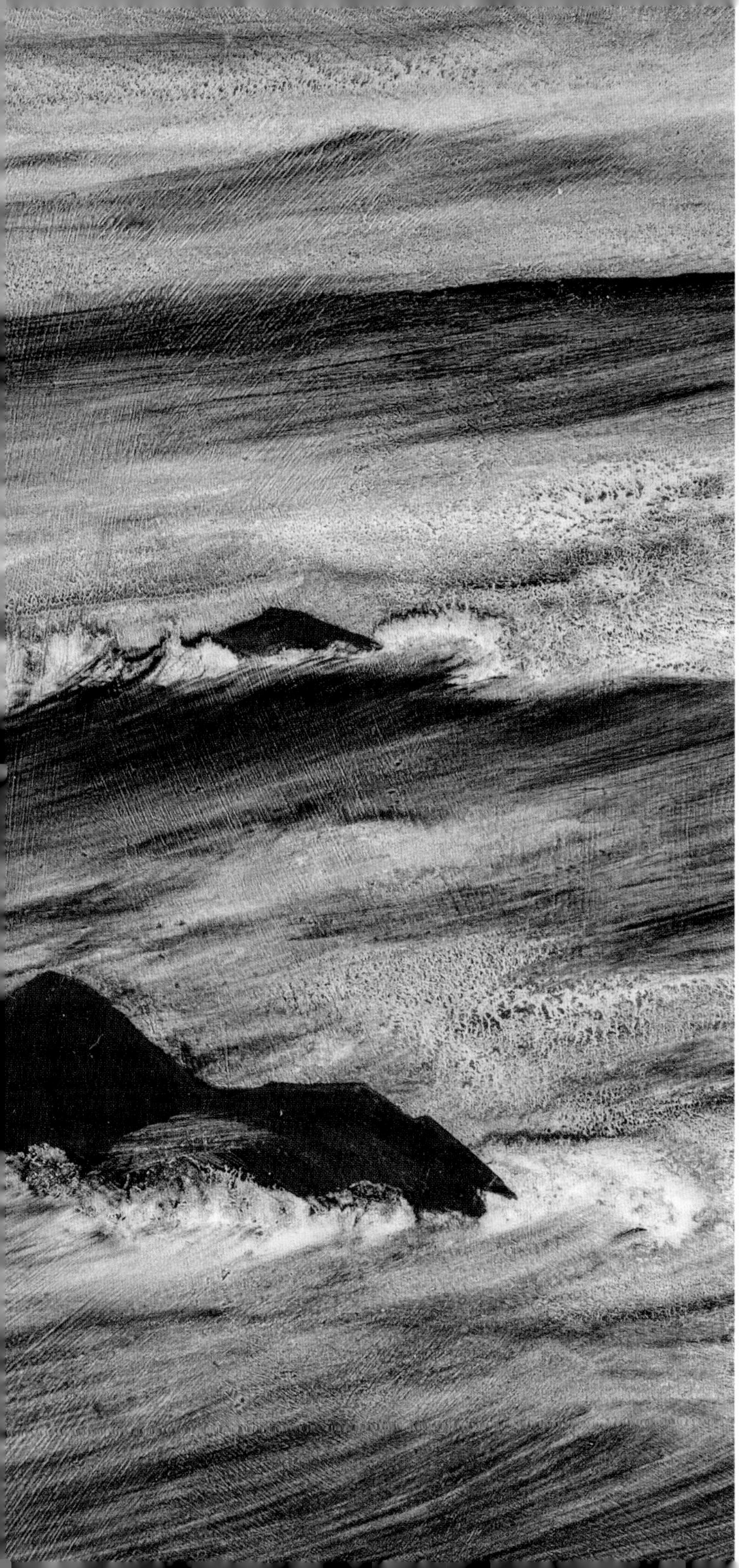

WAHINE

The 10th of April 1968 is forever etched into New Zealand history as the day the Wahine passenger ferry sank in Wellington harbour in a storm of hurricane strength; agonisingly, the Wahine was within a stone's throw of the shoreline but unreachable due to the mountainous seas. Fifty-three people died as a result of the sinking: this track is in memory of those people and this event, but also to the many other ships wrecked and lives lost in New Zealand waters.

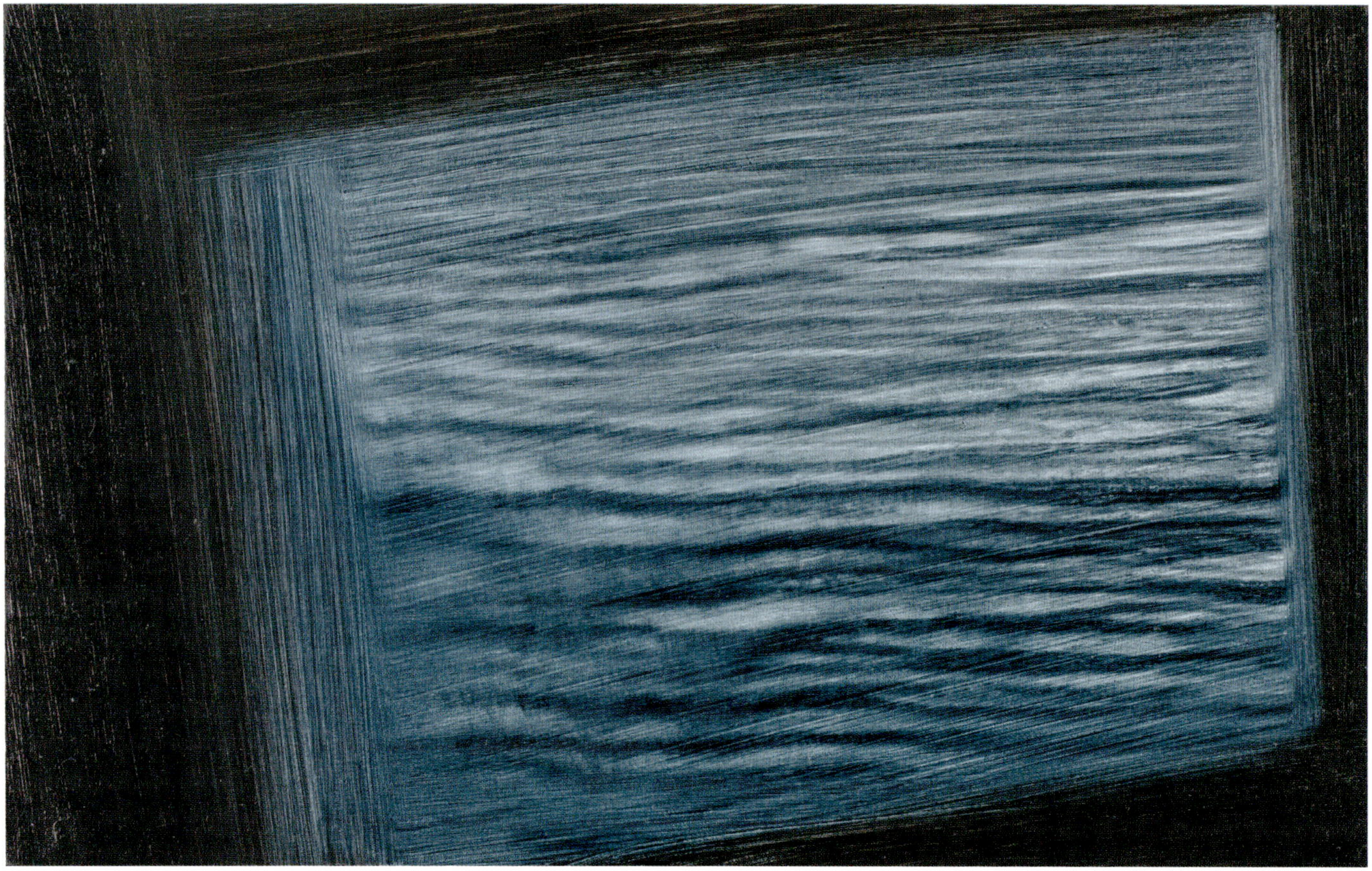

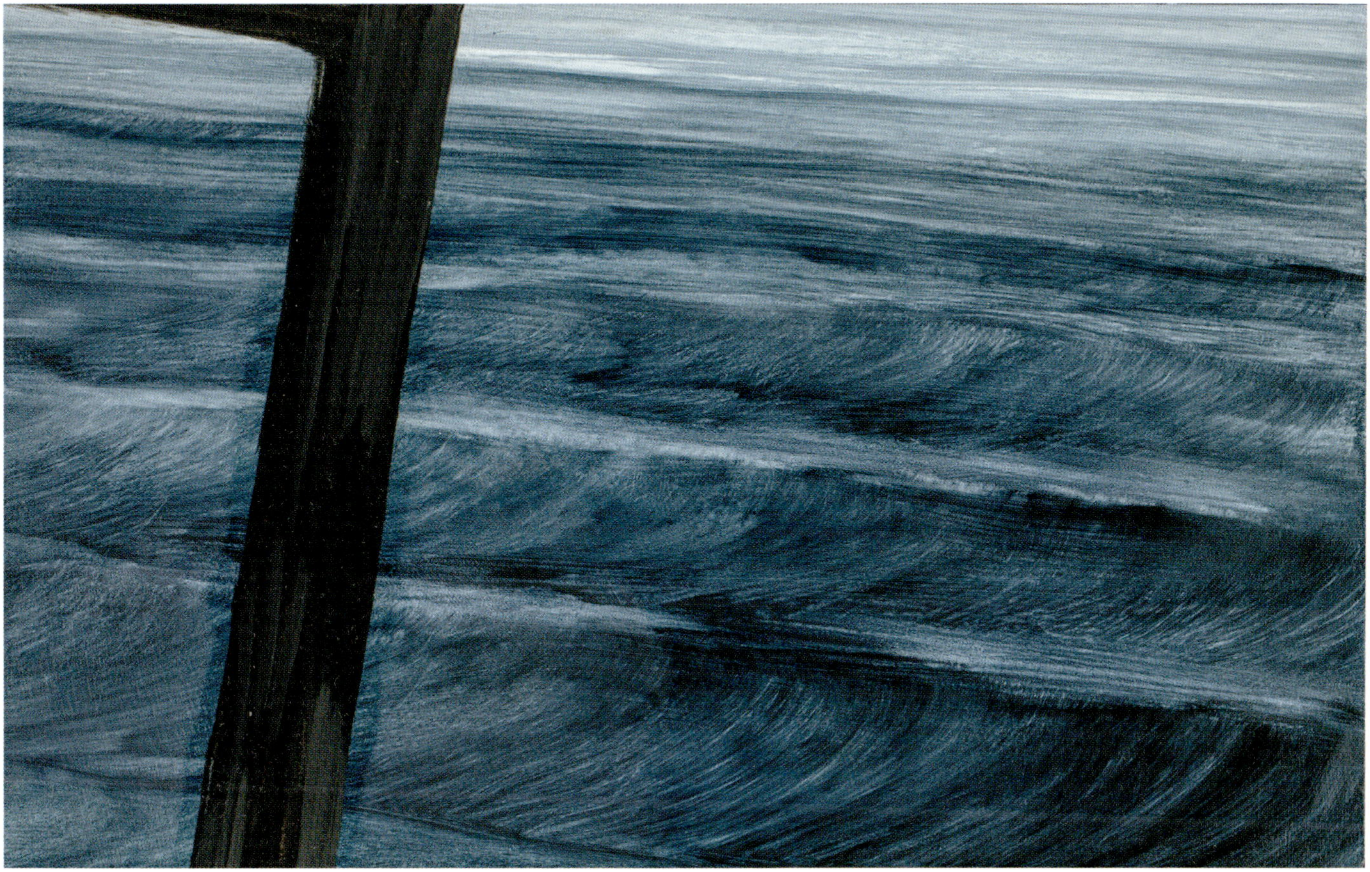

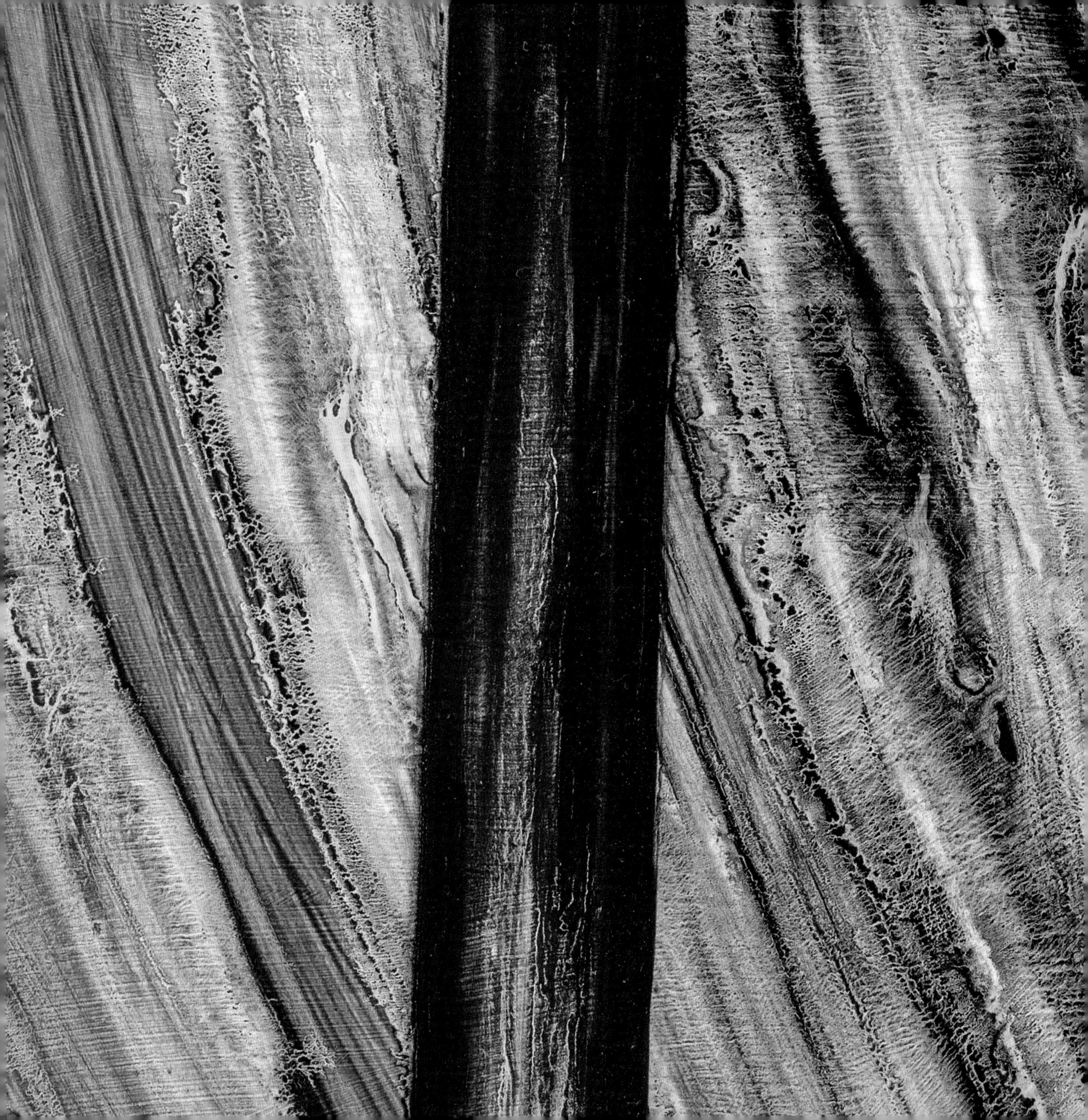

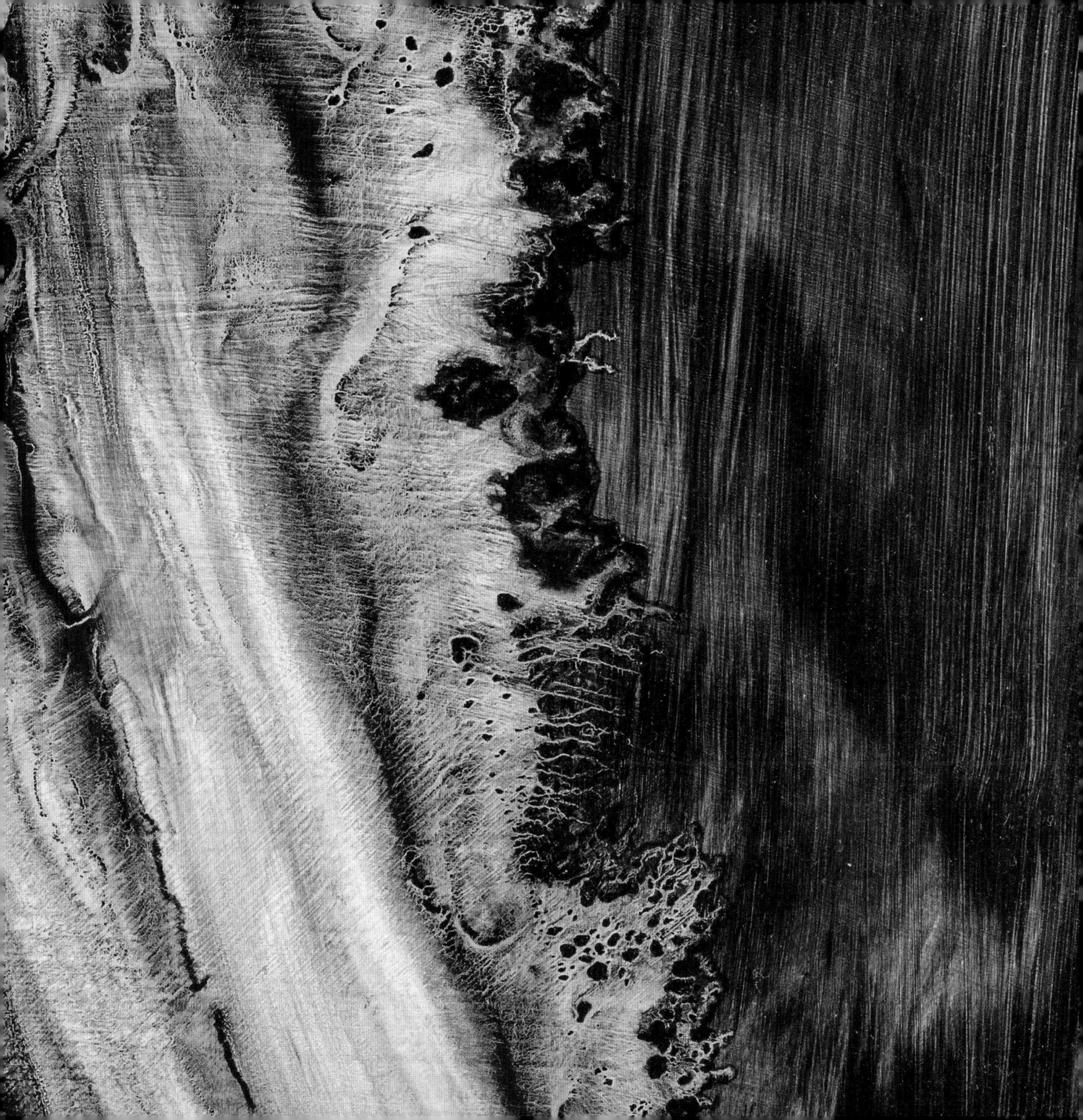

GLOSSARY

The Empire City: a common name for Wellington, coined by local residents and newspapers in the late 19th century. Sometimes 'the Empire City of the South Pacific'.

Ship Cove: A safe anchorage in Queen Charlotte Sound visited by James Cook on each of his three New Zealand voyages. Colonel William Wakefield's first landing point in New Zealand, on his way to establishing the colony of Wellington.

The New Zealand Company: A British company founded by William Wakefield's older brother, Edward, that sought to colonise New Zealand as a private venture. The Company made its money by reselling land purchased from local Māori. It started settlements in several locations including Wellington. It was strongly opposed to the Treaty of Waitangi and frequently in conflict with the British government.

Colonel William Wakefield: Commander of the first private expedition to colonise New Zealand.

Captain Arthur Wakefield: Younger brother of Edward and William. He was killed in 1843 during the Wairau Affray.

The Wairau Affray: A major conflict between British settlers and Māori that occurred on 17 June, 1843. Up to 26 people lost their lives, mainly British. Governor FitzRoy surprisingly (but correctly) ruled that the British had been largely at fault.

William Massey: One of New Zealand's longest-serving prime ministers. He was nicknamed 'Farmer Bill' due to his unwavering advocacy for rural interests.

The Union Steam Ship Company: Commercial shipping in New Zealand around the turn of the 20th century was dominated by the USS Company, which alternately engaged in cutthroat competition with its competitors or conspired to rig the shipping trade with them. Mark Twain once described its ferries as 'nothing more than cattle scows'.

1913 Great Strike: Arguably the most comprehensive labour strike in New Zealand's history. Tens of thousands of workers stopped work and the country was paralysed for weeks, resulting in major long-term law changes.

Jubilee Dock: Wellington's old floating dry dock. As a result of one too many labour disputes and plain old age, it was ultimately sold in 1988 and shipped off to South East Asia (but sank en route).

Richard Seddon: New Zealand politician from 1879 and Premier (1893–1906). A big man in every way, 'King Dick' was part of New Zealand politics for a quarter of a century and was a dominant figure in Wellington's and New Zealand's political landscape. His granddaughter Mary Seddon founded the famous Monde Marie coffee bar, one of the first in Wellington to feature poetry readings and folk music in the late 1950s.

The Public Trust: Established in the late 19th century to provide a secure public basis for estate management, it advertised its stability in New Zealand granite with the opening in 1908 of the impressive Public Trust office on Lambton Quay.

Pelorus Jack: A remarkable dolphin who escorted many vessels through the waters of Pelorus Sound to the entrance to French Pass in the early 1900s.

Athletic Park: Historic Wellington rugby ground, scene of many famous international test matches, and well known in the early days for its slippery muddy embankments.

The Māori Jesus: A poem by James K. Baxter highlighting the difficulty of being Māori living in Wellington in the late 1960s.

George Troup: Wellington's mayor from 1927–1931. His forward-thinking public construction projects helped guide the city in a positive way through the Depression years.

Fiddler's Green: A mythical place at the bottom of the sea where sailors end up 'if they don't go to hell'. The concept is originally attributed to Frederick Marryat and later became a well-known folk song by John Connolly.

The Leaving of Liverpool: A popular traditional song that, among other things, laments the hard life of a sailor.

Jock Cardnough: A familiar figure on Wellington's wharves for several decades and legend of oral anecdotal history.

The Cuba: Early immigrant ship that gave its name to Wellington's Cuba Street.

William Levin: Well-known Wellington businessman, provincial politician and public benefactor. Founding chairman of the Wellington Harbour Board in 1880. The town of Levin was named after him.

William Jackson: Chairman of the Wellington Harbour Board from 1881–1883. He arranged to lease Queens Wharf from the Wellington City Corporation so the port could be expanded.

Sir Thomas Wilford: Chairman of the Wellington Harbour Board from 1908–1910, member of Parliament, statesman and distinguished lawyer.

Harold Beauchamp: Chairman of the Wellington Harbour Board from 1900–1903, banker, and father of Katherine Mansfield.

William Cable: Chairman of the Wellington Harbour Board from 1904–1906. He emigrated from Scotland in 1869 and became a leading metal engineer.

Joseph Harkness: Chairman of the Wellington Harbour Board from 1919–1923.

John McEwan: Chairman of the Wellington Harbour Board from 1929–1931 and long-serving mayor of Petone.

Sir Charles Norwood: Chairman of the Wellington Harbour Board from 1931–1933 and a member of the board itself for an astonishing 35 years. Norwood was also the city mayor from 1925–1927 and founded the Wellington Milk Depot, the Fire Board and the Free Ambulance. The Wellington Botanic Garden's rose garden was named after his wife, Lady Norwood.

Wellington Harbour Board: Independent governing body of Wellington's wharves from 1880 till 1989, when it was replaced by three separate public bodies as part of nationwide restructuring.

Pollard and Sharps: A byproduct of wheat production, often fed to pigs and poultry.

The Midland Hotel: One of Wellington's grander hotels of the 20th century, its Spanish Mission-style building was a feature of Lambton Quay until it fell victim to the demolition derby of the late 1970s and 80s to make way for a new high-rise office block and Midland Park.

The Hunter Exchange: Early colonial exchange building that somehow survived unscathed until the 1970s, when it was demolished.

Chase Corporation: Property developers responsible for many of Wellington's new buildings in the 1970s and 80s, in many cases at the expense of older ones that were demolished. Chase itself collapsed in the late 80s during the global financial crisis.

LIST OF ILLUSTRATIONS

MUSICIANS

Andrew Laking – vocals, guitar, double bass
Justin Firefly – lead guitar (tracks 2, 5, 6, 7, 8)
Riki Gooch – drums (all tracks except 8, 10)
Petra Bullock – piano (tracks 1, 4, 5, 8, 9),
backing vocals (tracks 1, 7, 9)
Toby Laing – trumpet
Bret McKenzie – backing vocals (tracks 4, 6, 8)
Norman Meehan – piano (track 10)
Reece McNaughten – drums (tracks 3, 8)

Orchestra (arranged by Justin Firefly):
Robin Perks – violin
Sebastian Morgan-Lynch – cello
Heather Thompson – French horn
Bernard Wells – flute
Debbie Rawson – clarinet

Mixed by Andrew Laking and Robbie Duncan
Recorded and mastered by Robbie Duncan,
Braeburn Studios

Produced by Andrew Laking

Published by Pirate & Queen
pirateandqueen.co.nz
in association with Victoria University Press
PO Box 600 Wellington
vup.victoria.ac.nz

First published in August 2015

National Library of New Zealand Cataloguing-in-Publication Data
Laking, Andrew, 1974-
The Empire City / words, Andrew Laking;
Colour photographs, Ines MacMullen
Black and white photographs, Alexander Turnbull Library
Paintings, Bob Kerr

ISBN: 978-0-86473-990-2

Edited by Fergus Barrowman and Ashleigh Young

Design by Margaret Cochran
Layout by Geoff Norman
Printed by Everbest, China

THANKS TO:

The Museum of Wellington City & Sea,
Chris Maclean, Ben Weston for contribution to *Ship Song*, Rob Laking and Claire Mabey for editing help, Colleen, David & George Laking, Victor Young, Joe Bartley, Mark Derby, Chris & Margaret Cochran, Chris Price, Anthony Haas, Paul Thompson, Rachel Ingram, Tim Fraser for sourcing archival photos, John Gardiner, Gerry Paul, Chris Thornton and Ricoh, The New Zealand School of Music, all the musicians, designers and artists who provided so much life to this production, and all my family and friends.

This book was made possible with the assistance of Creative New Zealand.

creative nz
ARTS COUNCIL OF NEW ZEALAND TOI AOTEAROA